The Improv Comedy Musician

The Ultimate Guide to Playing Music with an Improv Group

Laura Hall and Bob Baker

Sister Trudy's Music

Los Angeles, CA

www.LauraHall.com • www.Bob-Baker.com

The Improv Comedy Musician

Published by Sister Trudy's Music
Box 4133, Valley Village, CA 91617

ISBN-13: 978-0692753408
ISBN-10: 0692753400

Cover design by Bob Baker. Cover art by Balabolka via Shutterstock.

Disclaimer

This book is designed to provide information on learning, rehearsing and performing musical improv. It is sold with the understanding that the publisher and authors are not engaged in rendering legal, accounting, or other professional services. If legal or other expert assistance is required, the services of a competent professional should be sought.

It is not the purpose of this book to cover the full range of information that is otherwise available on this topic, but instead to complement, amplify, and supplement other texts. You are urged to read all available material and tailor the information to your individual needs.

Every effort has been made to make this book as accurate as possible. However, some details may be inaccurate by the time you read this.

The author and publisher shall have neither liability nor responsibility to any person or entity with respect to any loss or damage caused, or alleged to have been caused, directly or indirectly, by the information contained in this book.

Dedications

Laura

To Rick, Eva, and Ruthie. I love and adore you!

And for Mom, my biggest fan!

Bob

To anyone who has ever faced their fear and dared to act and sing without a script.

And to my daughter Kelli, who taught me how to improvise being a proud and happy dad!

Contents

Section 3: It's Show Time – Now What?

Section 4: Working with Singers and Groups

Section 5: A Final Flurry of Musical Improv Goodness

Foreword

Laura Hall has written a book on musical improvisation. Obviously, since you're holding it in your hands.

What isn't so obvious, especially to regular viewers of *Whose Line Is It Anyway?*, is why (with all the incredible musical talent on that show) the performer most deficient in that department would be the one writing this Foreword.

It's like someone with a peanut allergy being asked to gush about Skippy.

Honestly, I am writing this because I truly believe that if you are going to learn something, learn from the best. Laura Hall is simply one of the best practitioners of the art of musical improvisation.

Consider these five facts:

1) Laura worked for The Second City, the historic institution that developed most of the people you have ever laughed at on stage or on screen. The Second City hires top-notch talent, and that includes its musical directors.

Not only are musicians like Laura in charge of providing original music or parodies for the cast, they also play a soundtrack to each scene, adding emotional content, musical jokes, etc. That is experience you can't get anywhere else.

2) On *Whose Line*, Laura supplies note-perfect music styles for Wayne Brady, Brad Sherwood, Chip Esten, Jeff Davis, et al, to shine on. But let's face it, with those guys the workload is cut by a healthy percentage. Laura's true genius is that she can make caterwaulers like me sound good and, more important, makes caterwaulers like me feel safe enough to try.

In improvisation, trust is paramount between the cast members, and nowhere is that more needed than in the musical arena. When I perform a song with Laura, even the dreaded "Hoedown," the music is clear enough that I can follow it.

And, when I need it the most, Laura follows me so I can get my panic-fueled rhymes out. She knows how to get the best out of everyone!

3) Laura has taught musical improv across the US and Canada. Everyone I have talked to who has taken the classes – novices and veterans alike – are amazed at the progress they made in a few short hours. Why would it be different for you?

4) There is no musical style that Laura isn't versed in and, believe me, on the show we've thrown everything at her – from Japanese pop to opera to a Christopher Walken/Amy Winehouse duet. She's unflappable.

5) Laura Hall is a damn fine musician, period. She has recorded children's records, solo albums, two volumes of *Improv Karaoke*, and CDs with her band, The Sweet Potatoes – all of which I highly recommend. (No royalties needed for me, Laura.)

With Laura Hall you get experience, knowledge, and a teacher you can trust. What more could you ask for? So get reading, start playing, and have more fun than you're ready for.

Just stay away from "Hoedown." Trust me.

–Colin Mochrie

Laura with Colin, in Las Vegas, 2011

A Note From Guitarist Linda Taylor

Playing music is about finding a balance between loud and soft, fast and slow, empty space and dense orchestration.

Being a musician on *Whose Line Is It Anyway?* is all about finding your balance. On a tightrope. In outer space. With two broken legs. While being shot at by alien aircraft. As a stagehand runs a vacuum cleaner. With the A/C permanently set to 40 degrees.

Laura Hall and I have worked together for nearly 20 years. Our paths hadn't crossed prior to *Whose Line*, which is weird because female musicians are still somewhat of a rarity; we tend to know each other.

I was aware of Laura because of the show. I enjoyed watching the first season of the American version (she had a glorious year all by herself). I always marveled at how easily she and Wayne Brady would just toss off musical styles. How did they do Prince? She didn't even play a guitar on the show! They made it sound just like the late, great musical genius from Minneapolis. Wow!

I auditioned with Laura and Wayne in a dance studio. (Because, if you're going to crank up a guitar amp, a mirrored room with no PA system is just the place you wanna be.)

Dan Patterson, the producer and co-creator of the show, was there and called out styles. I was impressed with how easily Laura and I pulled something together. Actually, she pulled something together and yelled chords at me, but it still sounded good. Besides, she needed me for metal, punk, "obnoxious guitar," and "loud."

Laura's depth and breadth of experience with The Second City and her background in improv is more than evident. She just knows how to shape music into something that perfectly supports this bizarre format.

The key to our *Whose Line* gig is really understanding the role that music plays in the show, and Laura is the queen of that skill. She knows exactly how a song is going to function within the show, and then we apply "reductive surgery," as she calls it.

Laura taught me to ask these important questions:

- What is it about this particular style that makes it "it"?
- Is it a beat or a tempo?
- Is it an instrument?
- What's the one thing we can immediately play that Wayne (or whoever is singing) can latch on to?
- How can we help our singers do their job?

It's interesting, because in musical improv, we have to draw upon all of our experience and vocabulary ... then, just as quickly, be willing to let it go.

I'm extremely proud of what we do on *Whose Line*. I know, it's all a joke, but I'm still impressed when Laura and I spontaneously nail something, as if we've been playing it for years.

Working together, we've both expanded our musical range and knowledge a great deal. I now know who Brecht is (it's not an old shampoo brand) and Laura owns a Tupac song or two (thanks to my influence).

We've got a vocabulary that is so balanced and thorough, I know we'll always find something to play, something close enough, something immediate.

We will find it and you will laugh. Hopefully, for many years in syndication.

Linda Taylor (left) and Laura on the *Whose Line* set

Introduction

I'll never forget the moment I was onstage with Robin Williams and suddenly felt completely helpless and filled with terror.

I had been hired to lead a band for a big awards show at the El Portal Theatre in Los Angeles. The musicians and I played while the audience came in and for walk-ons and walk-offs during the show.

Robin was there to present a lifetime achievement award to his hero, Jonathan Winters. It was a big deal – a highlight of the evening.

Not surprisingly, during his segment Robin started riffing and effortlessly slid into his evangelical preacher character. Knowing I did improv, he turned to me and said, "Let's sing a little gospel, sister."

So far so good. But here's the thing: He was wearing a clip-on mic, which was not coming through my stage monitor. That meant, while he was facing me, I could hear him fine. But once he turned toward the audience, and I started playing (with my keyboard fully in my monitor), I couldn't hear him sing at all.

I felt like I was dangling on a high wire – completely without a net. We had never improvised together before. But there he was singing, gesturing, and whipping the crowd into a frenzy. And there I was helplessly unable to hear him.

How could I possibly follow and support this iconic performer under these circumstances?

That's when adrenaline and instinct kicked in. Even though I couldn't hear Robin, I could *see* him. So I watched how he moved and paid attention to the pace of his breathing. I tried my best to read his body language to get a feel for how he was phrasing things musically.

In essence, I used my gut and years of experience to guide me as I played along with him. Afterward, Robin turned and gave me a big smile and a thumbs up. I guess I did okay. Crisis averted.

I tell this story because it speaks to one of the challenges of teaching what I and other improv musicians do. It's the main reason I put off writing a book like this for years.

Even though I've taught improv workshops for singers for a long time, I've always struggled with articulating exactly how a musician should learn improv. Why? Because the answer always comes back to "follow your instincts."

It was instinct that allowed me to accompany Robin Williams under those adverse conditions. It was instinct that allowed me to hone my craft with The Second City, The Annoyance Theater, and many other performing groups over the years. And it was instinct that helped me land a sweet TV gig on *Whose Line Is It Anyway?*

With that in mind, here are my first three tips for becoming an excellent improv comedy musician:

- First, get a lot of experience playing a wide variety of styles.
- Second, be open-minded and flexible – not only in how you structure the music you play but also with the career path you follow.

- And third, trust the instincts you develop from doing the first two things.

That's it.

Of course, we're not going to end the book here. Even though I was reluctant before, I now realize there is a lot of wisdom I can pass on from my decades of musical improv experience.

We all have skills we take for granted because they are second nature to us. We're so close to them, we may not realize the value they have for others. Writing this book has forced me to look at this delicate art of musical improv with fresh eyes. I'm excited to break it down for you and share my insights into what makes the musical aspects of improv work.

Another important point: What you see me do on *Whose Line* is just a tiny slice of what musicians can do in a live improv show. Your role includes a lot more than simply accompanying singers. Your creativity and imagination are the only limits. In this book I'll share a wide range of ways you can contribute to an improv show and have fun doing it.

More good news: Whether you want to do this just for fun or as a working musician, most improv groups will be thrilled to have you. Musicians are in short supply in the improv world, especially players who are well versed at it. And often we're the only one in the group who gets paid!

For these reasons and more, I'm thrilled to share what I've learned.

I'm also grateful to work with Bob Baker, a gifted writer and musician with years of book publishing and improv experience. His input and guidance were an immense help in organizing and clarifying all of the best practices we cover throughout the book.

Of course, the best way to learn is by doing. But if we can give you a roadmap and some direction along the way, I hope it shortens the learning curve toward your goal of being an improv musician.

Learning to play for improv has been one of the most exciting, freeing and surprising parts of my musical life. It has improved my musicianship and ear. It's made me a more fluid, versatile, brave and flexible musician in all contexts. And it's gotten me lots of work.

I hope your life is equally blessed with music and improv.

–Laura Hall

Laura enjoys a *Whose Line* standing ovation at the Adelphi Theatre in London

Laura's Long, Strange Trip Through Music and Improv

You probably know me best as the music director and piano player on *Whose Line Is It Anyway?* But my story goes a lot deeper than that. If you're curious about my musical background and how I got into doing improv, this section is for you.

During my junior year of college I got a job at The Second City in Chicago as a coat check girl, which led to a promotion as a waitress. Since I grew up in Chicago, I had seen improv, but I never planned on being an improv musician. In those days I spent my time working, going to school, studying composition and music theory, and writing songs.

I also stayed busy playing at church services and dance classes, as well as piano bars, in the pit band for musicals, in wedding bands, original music bands, and more. (Little did I know how much all of these varied experiences would come in handy later.)

When I waited tables at The Second City, the legendary Fred Kaz played piano for the main stage shows. He served as music director there for 24 years. I admit, I was a terrible waitress. I would deliver drinks and then get totally distracted by the amazing ways Fred played. I got completely hooked and enamored of improv, especially the musician's role in it.

In those days the performers and staff would often hang out after the venue closed and I would sometimes play the piano. Word got around that I was a decent musician. The Second City was expanding with touring shows and corporate gigs, so I was offered a job as a fill-in improv musician. I took it. (I often joke that I was "demoted" to musician, since the waitresses made a lot more money.)

I learned the ropes doing one-nighters on the road. Before long I was assigned to an official Second City Touring Company. That's how you earned your stripes as a performer: You honed your skills in a Touring Company, doing about 80% proven sketch comedy and 20% improv. If you did well and there was an opening, you got promoted to a resident company, where you got to develop your own material. From there, you might get noticed and move on to *Saturday Night Live* or TV or movie roles.

My improv love connection

One of the actors in the Touring Company was a handsome and funny guy named Rick Hall. We got to know each other and managed to fall in love while touring the country in what can be best described as a crowded, stinky van. (Sadly, the life of a touring improv group is not all that glamorous.)

Rick eventually got promoted to the main stage and I moved up to open a show on Second City's new e.t.c. stage. Leaving the close quarters of the Touring Company gave our relationship room to grow, and we ended up getting married.

Once I got involved with improv, I was hooked. In addition to The Second City, I also performed at other Chicago venues, including The Improv Institute, The Annoyance Theatre, Improv Olympic, and any improv group that would have me.

Soon after we were married, Rick got an acting job in Los Angeles. We decided to move to California for one year to see how we felt about it. That was more than two decades ago, so I guess it worked out for us.

When we moved to LA I decided to take a break from improv. I spent a few years focusing on songwriting, playing in original bands, writing musicals, and learning to score movies and TV shows. Rick and I also had our first baby.

Then life took an unexpected turn when I got a call from Ron West, one of my old Second City Touring Company friends. He asked if I wanted to audition for a TV show called *Whose Line Is It Anyway?* Of course, I did, and my life has been blessed immensely ever since.

A quick *Whose Line* history lesson

In case you don't know the story, here's a brief look at the life and times of the show. *Whose Line Is It Anyway?* was created by Dan Patterson and Mark Leveson in 1988 as a radio show on BBC Radio. Six episodes aired.

Later that year the show moved to television on Channel 4, a British public-service station. This TV version of *Whose Line* aired for 10 seasons and produced 136 episodes, all of which were hosted by Clive Anderson.

Some familiar American performers appeared on the British version, including Ryan Stiles, Colin Mochrie, Brad Sherwood, Greg Proops, and Chip (aka Charles) Esten.

Ryan Stiles was instrumental in bringing the show to the United States. He had a regular role on *The Drew Carey Show*, which was very popular in the late 1990s. Ryan pitched the idea to Drew, who loved the idea and persuaded ABC to air test episodes in the U.S.

The British version of *Whose Line* was heading into its last season. To help make the transition from one side of the Atlantic to the other, the tenth and final season of the British show was recorded in Los Angeles. Clive Anderson sat behind the desk, but it featured an all-American cast.

In 1998 I was hired for these "hybrid" shows. I auditioned with Wayne Brady, who the producers had discovered in Florida, and Brad Sherwood. They felt Wayne was the secret weapon for the new American version. That certainly proved to be right. We all got the gig and, lo and behold, I was doing improv again! (I'll tell you more about auditioning for *Whose Line* later in the book.)

That same year we started recording the American version on ABC, with Drew Carey at the helm. It ran successfully for eight seasons. We produced nearly 200 episodes through 2006. It was a blast!

Over those years I had the pleasure of performing with the amazing regular cast members, in addition to celebrity guests such as Robin Williams, Kathy Griffin, Whoopi Goldberg, Sid Caesar, Stephen Colbert, David Hasselhoff, Florence Henderson, Jerry Springer, and Richard Simmons.

The hiatus and rebirth of *Whose Line*

By the time the ABC version of the show came to a close, Rick and I were raising two daughters. Over the next few years I focused on being a mom, while also doing movie scores, playing in bands, and staying active with improv in Los Angeles. At various times I sat in with the Groundlings, iO West (formerly Improv Olympic), ComedySportz, Theatresports, and Totally Looped.

In addition to short-form improv, I played music for a lot of long-form formats too, including Harolds and Armandos. I sat in with Opening Night: The Improvised Musical, creating full-length musicals based on one audience suggestion. And, using improv, I created scripted musicals with Theater-A-Go-Go.

I toured with Drew Carey's Improv All Stars doing live shows all over the country. (This time I wasn't cramped in a stinky van; we toured in a big rock-band-style tour bus!)

Like I said, *Whose Line* is just one tiny sliver of the musical improv work I've done over the years.

During these hiatus years I founded a trio called The Sweet Potatoes with Kelly Macleod and my husband Rick. We play original, acoustic, Americana-style music with three-part harmonies. In this ensemble (my personal pride and joy) I write, sing and play the guitar, ukulele and accordion, which gives me a whole new perspective as a musician.

I also created *Improv Karaoke*, a two-CD set with karaoke style tracks for doing song improv. It includes tutorials and demos by some of my improviser friends, including Keegan-Michael Key (of *Key & Peele*, *Playing House*, and *Mad TV*) and Dan Castellaneta (who does the voice of Homer and many other characters on *The Simpsons*). In addition, Rick and I started teaching music improv workshops for actors and singers.

After years of hearing rumors that *Whose Line* would be back on the air, I got a call from executive producer Dan Patterson. In 2013, the show returned to the airwaves on the CW Network, featuring a new host, the hilarious and energetic Aisha Tyler. Most of the regular cast returned, including accomplished guitarist Linda Taylor, who has been my *Whose Line* musical partner since the second season on ABC.

As I write this, we just finished recording the fourth season of the CW incarnation, and we're getting ready to do a second run of *Whose Line Live* in London, with a combined cast from the British and American television shows.

I feel so blessed to have had the pleasure to work with Jeff Davis, Keegan-Michael Key, Gary Anthony Williams, Heather Anne Campbell, Nyima Funk, and Jonathan Mangum. Not to mention more celebrity guests such as Cedric the Entertainer, Kathie Lee Gifford, Penn & Teller, Bill Nye, Sheryl Hines, and Verne Troyer.

Yes, it's been a rich life filled with music and improv. And there's no sign of things slowing down any time soon.

The Second City Touring Company. Back row, left to right: Laura (with an unfortunate 1980s haircut), Will Clinger, Christina Dunne, Sean Masterson. Front row: Ron West, Judith Scott, Tim O'Malley, Evan Gore

Laura with her band, Trinket, in the 1990s

Laura on a USO tour with Drew Carey's Improv All Stars

On the *Whose Line* set (left to right): Wayne Brady, Jonathan Mangum, Aisha Tyler, Colin Mochrie, Ryan Stiles, Laura Hall, Linda Taylor, and Dan Patterson

What About Bob?

Even though Laura and I didn't meet until fairly recently, we both share Midwest roots. I was born and raised in St. Louis, Missouri, about five hours south of Chicago by car. Being a river town along the Mississippi, St. Louis has a long history of music and culture, including improv.

In the late 1950s the Compass Players performed at the Crystal Palace in an area called Gaslight Square in St. Louis. They thrilled audiences with a fresh form of entertainment known as improvisational theatre. The performers included Mike Nichols, Elaine May, Del Close, Ted Flicker, and Paul Sills. During these Gaslight Square years the group developed a set of principles to guide improvisational actors.

After the Compass Players disbanded in 1959, Paul Sills returned to Chicago and founded The Second City. Even though this all happened before I was born, I'm proud that my hometown played an important role in improv history.

As for my own career path, it's been rich with music and performance activities. I started playing guitar and singing with rock bands in high school. Over the decades I've performed everything from classic rock and Top 40 to alternative and original music. If it rocked, popped or grooved, I played some form of it.

I never had formal music training. I learned to play by ear and through collaborating with many talented musicians. When writing original music, I would create a chord pattern or groove, then improvise vocally over it until I came up with a melody I liked. Later I'd craft lyrics to fit the melody and feel of the song, using different rhyming patterns. Little did I know how much these skills would serve me when I eventually did improv.

Making it up as you go

In my mid twenties, my friend Lee Mueller and I were big fans of *Saturday Night Live* and had heard that most of *SNL*'s cast members had backgrounds in improv. He and I would often take a home video camera and improvise scenes and fake documentaries for fun.

In 1985 I made a trip to Canada, where I caught a show at The Second City in Toronto. I was fascinated by the sketch comedy/improv format. That same year Lee and I formed our first improv troupe in St. Louis with some of our actor friends. I was hooked.

In the decades since, I've done a lot of creative things: performed stand-up comedy, acted in dozens of plays, directed plays, written and performed sketch comedy, and published a local music magazine. In my early thirties, my first book was published, which led to my primary career as an author and independent book publisher.

Over the years I've developed a solid reputation as a music marketing expert and an advocate for self-publishers and creative people of all kinds. Some of my books include *The Guerrilla Music Marketing Handbook*, *The Five-Minute Music Marketer*, *Branding Yourself Online*, *The Guerrilla Guide to Book Marketing*, *The Empowered Artist*, and *Unleash the Artist Within*.

Even though I continued to do improv off and on over the years, in 2011 I got back into it in a big way. I started teaching and performing short-form improv, taking classes myself (the wisest people are both teachers and students), and adding more music to my improv bag of tricks.

The show where everything's made up and the points don't matter

Like a lot of improvisers and comedy buffs, I'm a huge fan of *Whose Line Is It Anyway?* I've probably seen most of the episodes. In 2014, when Laura and her husband Rick came to St. Louis to teach an improv workshop, it was a no-brainer. I signed up immediately.

The night of the afternoon workshop I performed with ten other students in front of a lively audience. I must admit, it was surreal to sing on stage and look down to see Laura's familiar face behind the keyboard. "Oh my God," I thought. "Laura Hall is accompanying me in a live improv show!" (I know, I'm starting to sound like a fanboy.)

In 2015, I reached out to Laura and asked if she'd like to be a guest on my "Creative Entrepreneur" podcast. She was gracious enough to do the interview. Afterwards, she asked a simple question about my books. During that conversation the idea of writing a book together was born.

Like many of the best things in life, this collaboration came about unexpectedly and organically – while pursuing something that brings great joy to my life. It doesn't get much better than that.

Working on this book and getting to know Laura and Rick has been a real blessing. I hope this resource informs and inspires you to use your musical gifts in a way that will add richness and laughter to your life and the lives of countless others who are exposed to it.

Rock on!

Bob (far right) performs the Blues Torpedoes with
(left to right) Theresa Masters, Tim Hill, and Karen Schubert.

About This Book

Now that we've covered some important preliminary info, we're about to dive into the meat of the book. Before we move ahead, here are a few things you need to know ...

This book is about the art of musical improv. More specifically, it's about the role that music and musicians play in an improv comedy ensemble, whether that ensemble performs short form, long form, or some other improv format.

It's especially helpful for any musician who:

- is thinking of joining or starting an improv group
- has just joined a group and wants to learn the craft
- is already a member of an improv group and wants to sharpen their skills

You'll also get a lot of value from the book if you are an improv teacher, a coach, or the musical or creative director of an improv group. The insight you'll get in the following pages will help you know what to look for in a good improv musician. It will also give you the tools to guide your musician to be a better team player.

While this isn't a book about improv singing or acting per se, both singers and actors will benefit a great deal. Getting a peek behind the veil of how music supports and enhances an improv show will give you a strong perspective you can use to develop and grow as a player. Plus, reading about Laura's background and the inner workings of *Whose Line Is It Anyway?* will be an entertaining read.

What's ahead?

We've structured the book in a way that makes the most sense to us.

Section 1, "Setting the Stage," gives you an overview of the history of improv, some basic principles, and a rundown of the forms you are likely to encounter as a musician. You'll definitely want to read this if you're new to improv or want to get a solid foundation to build upon.

Section 2, "The Heart and Soul of Musical Improv," is the meat of this topic. Practically everything you need to know about the role of music in an improv show is here: transitions, underscoring, improvising songs, and much more.

Section 3, "It's Show Time – Now What?" This section takes a step back and covers your gear options, pre-show checklist, stage positioning, warm-up exercises, etc.

Section 4, "Working with Singers and Groups," helps you navigate the waters of working with singers and being a coveted team player.

Section 5, "A Final Flurry of Musical Improv Goodness," has Laura answering your most pressing *Whose Line* questions, along with a list of improv resources, final thoughts, and more.

Our point of view

The challenge with creating a book by two authors is letting the reader know who is talking (or writing) at any given time. Do we reference ourselves from a distance third-person point of view? ("Laura does this, Bob does that.") Or do we speak directly from a first-person perspective? ("My favorite way to play songs is ...")

Here's the solution we came up with:

The majority of the book is written in third-person. However, some stories just scream to be told from a first-person point of view. These first-person sections will be set apart in italics with a heading that reads something like ...

Laura on the need to write in first person ...

I think it's really important that you know when I'm telling a riveting story from my life. So I'll present those riveting first-person accounts in riveting italics like this.

See how this works? Are you riveted?

Now that we've got these important housekeeping matters out of the way, let's dive into the wonderful world of musical improv!

Section 1

Setting the Stage

Before we jump into the mechanics of musical improv, let's take a minute to build a solid foundation. It helps to know where all of this improv stuff came from and what it's built upon.

Please join us on a quick journey through the history of improv, the basic principles that power it, and the formats you are likely to encounter along the way.

Welcome to a Grand Tradition

When you take on the role of a musician in an improv group, you become part of a long, rich history. For many thousands of years, people have used sound and music to support a wide range of public activities. From tribal rituals and religious ceremonies to celebrations and more, music has played an integral part in human events since before recorded history.

Music combined with improvised acting goes back at least 500 years. Roving groups of performers traveled across Europe in the 16th Century doing a form of theatre now known as commedia dell'arte. Performers wore masks and were required to both act and sing.

The tradition continued with Vaudeville and the work of Viola Spolin in the 1940s. The improv exercises she developed became the cornerstone of modern improv training. Spolin's son, Paul Sills, co-founded the Compass Players in the 1950s, which led to the birth of The Second City in Chicago. David Shepherd, Elaine May, Ted Flicker, and Del Close are just a few of the prominent people who propelled the art form in the 1960s.

In the 1970s, Keith Johnstone published the book *Impro*, which launched a style of improv comedy called Theatresports. Its popularity influenced the ComedySportz franchise and the format of the show *Whose Line Is It Anyway?* in the 1980s.

In more recent decades, the art form has continued to evolve as innovative actors, directors and musicians find new ways to use improv. There's short-form (like the fast-moving games you see on *Whose Line*) and long-form improv (such as Harolds and Armandos), practiced by Upright Citizens Brigade and many other groups.

Then there's puppet-prov (such as Brian Henson's Puppet Up), entire improvised musicals, and style-based improv shows (fashioned after a Shakespeare play, Sondheim musical, *Gilligan's Island* episode, etc.). Plus, the scripted scenes and sketch comedy you see at The Second City or on *Saturday Night Live* are often developed using improv.

Improv has even been used in film and television. Some popular examples include Christopher Guest's mockumentary films *This Is Spinal Tap* and *A Mighty Wind*, as well as Larry David's *Curb Your Enthusiasm*.

So here we are today, as the story continues to unfold. Improv comedy classes, groups and shows have flourished and are growing in popularity.

Make no mistake, as a musician who supports improv, you are continuing a distinguished and longstanding art form.

The role of music in improv

Music in an improv show can serve many functions. We'll cover them in depth in upcoming sections. But to give you a quick summary, here are the three main roles that music plays in an improv comedy show:

1) Transitions – such as opening and closing the show, and playing between scenes or games to keep the energy moving and tie everything together.

2) Underscoring – like the score of a movie, music can heighten the emotions of a scene, help establish the place and time, and add energy and motion.

3) Accompanying improvised songs – sometimes called "songprov," this is done in games where you play music behind a singer (such as "Irish Drinking Song" or the game Greatest Hits). Song accompaniment can also happen within a scene or throughout an entire improvised musical.

One important thing improv musicians must understand is that the music is not always at the forefront of a show. In fact, much of the time, what you play will be a subtle background component of the overall game or scene.

The good news is, even when audience members aren't conscious of it, the music can add immensely to the energy and rhythm of the performance.

The not so good news is, it often feels as though people don't appreciate the musician as much as they do the "acting" performers. You need to be okay with this. First and foremost, the musician member of the group is a team player, always in service of the game or scene at hand.

But let's face it. Not all musicians enjoy taking this background role. If you're a player who needs to be out front, then you should play in a band or as a solo artist to get your fix in the spotlight. Then return to your role as a support player with your improv group.

Don't get the wrong idea. There will times in a show when you'll make a bold choice and be noticed and appreciated by your cast and the audience. Plus, a good host will give the musician lots of recognition and love. However, it's important that you know up front that your primary purpose as an improv musician is to support the players, games and scenes in ways that are often understated.

Laura on knowing the musical part she plays ...

I enjoy playing both roles. I love being part of the fabric of an improv show, but I also love being out front when I play and sing with my band, The Sweet Potatoes. They're two different animals, and it's important to understand the difference.

The Sweet Potatoes: Laura, Kelly Macleod (center) and Rick Hall

Improv Acting Rules and How They Apply to Music

An improv musician needs to be connected to the actors at all times during a show, just as the actors need to be connected to each other and the musician.

Therefore, if you haven't done so already, we highly recommend you take some improv classes to learn the basics of improv. This will give you a greater understanding of what the actors are doing.

What follows are some improv acting fundamentals that will come in handy as you ease into your role as an improv musician.

Yes, and ...

This is the foundation of improv and usually the first principle taught to new improv actors. The premise is simple: Improv is based on "agreement." When a new piece of information (often called an "offer") is introduced into a game or scene, it is automatically accepted as reality by the other player or players.

An offer can be verbal, as in "Help me lift this giant pink flamingo" or "Hey dad, I need to borrow the car keys." It can be physical, such as someone silently acting like they are washing the dishes, folding laundry, or walking with a limp. An offer can also be sound based, like a cough, a loud sigh, or yes, even a piece of music.

Once an actor or musician makes an "offer," the other actors in the scene must "yes, and" the offer. That means they immediately accept the new reality and add something concrete to move the scene forward.

Example:

Actor 1: "Help me lift this giant pink flamingo."

Actor 2: "Honey, this is the third pink flamingo you've brought home this week. You really need to stop going to yard sales."

The response from Actor 2 acknowledges Actor 1's offer and adds another element that clarifies what's going on in the scene.

For a musician, the process is similar. Your job is to both give and accept offers.

If an actor establishes that he's at a Renaissance Faire, it's your chance to play something from that era as underscore. Remember, you'll be faking it. You don't have to know an entire 16th Century motet. Just play something that hints at what you're trying to establish. For example, you might noodle on something like "Greensleeves."

The music can help establish the feel and mood, as well as the location. If the setting is a hospital waiting room, what would the scene be like if you made the first offer and played something frantic? Or boring? Or sad? Any of those choices could work, and they would certainly affect how the actors played the scene that followed.

In the Renaissance Faire scene, the actor made an offer and what the musician played was a "yes, and" to that offer. In the hospital scene, the musician made the offer, and it's up to the actors to "yes, and" in whatever way it inspires them.

That process continues throughout the scene, not just at the beginning. The mood may shift and the underscore music can help heighten the emotion.

Laura on the need to practice improv ...

People often ask, "How do you rehearse improv, since it's all made up?" Another common question is, "Why are there rules for improv? Isn't it all about breaking the rules?"

Both questions show how little people know about the heart of improv. Practicing improv is how we become better listeners, get out of our own heads, and learn to trust other players and our own instincts.

Regarding the "rules," I consider improv principles to be timeless guidelines for working well together.

Here's another benefit to "learning" improv: I think of all human beings as toddlers, no matter what their age. We all have to learn to share, listen, and get along with each other.

Like toddlers, we have an inherent sense of playfulness, endless amounts of creativity, and our own unique perspective. As we get older and become "adults" we often lose touch with our childlike nature and instinct.

Improv helps us reconnect with the sense of play that is at the heart of who we are.

Active listening

Another important principle of improv acting is referred to as "active" listening. A lot of novice players make the mistake of getting into their heads and trying to think of something clever to say. When an actor does that, he misses out on the offers and details being presented by his fellow players.

The ideal way to do improv is to be fully present in a scene and listen to your partner. Intensely observe her words, emotions, physical posture, and more. Then respond appropriately in the moment. Bob often tells his improv students, "Get out of your head and get into the moment."

Musicians would do well to embrace this principle too. Don't think ahead or force some musical concept you conjured up 30 seconds ago. Let go of any attachment to a scene's direction or outcome. Listen intently and be prepared to support what's happening right now in the scene.

The process really boils down to becoming adept at both leading and following, giving and taking. Sometimes you are following and supporting the actors; other times they are following your lead and reacting to the sonic changes you create.

This is especially true when you improvise songs together. Usually the musician establishes the key, rhythmic feel, and style right from the start. However, occasionally a brave actor will start singing a cappella, and you'll have to quickly figure out the key if you want to accompany them. Or, you might choose to have them do the whole song a cappella if that feels right.

Even when you start the action, you still have to follow the actors. This can be challenging if you have a chord progression or song structure in mind, and they go somewhere else. Your job is to go with them, even if they do something like come in after three and a half bars, when you thought it should be four.

Musical improv is sometimes compared to jazz – where the musicians play off of each other and take turns playing solos and being the focus. In some ways improv is like jazz, but in other ways it isn't. Because, even though a jazz musician is improvising, the chord structure is usually preset. Improv musicians create the chord structure and form as they go.

Laura on making strong choices ...

When I first started years ago with the Touring Company at The Second City, I lacked confidence and was too uncertain to make many offers. I mostly tried to stay out of the way of the actors and not make any "mistakes." But that was the wrong mindset.

The late Fred Kaz, the legendary music director at The Second City for 24 years, whom I learned so much from, once said to me, "If there are six actors on stage, you're the seventh improviser. You need to take your place."

So I got more assertive with my musical offers and the choices I made. And he was right. Fred, who was renowned for his ability to both lead and follow scenes, was always right.

Laura with Fred Kaz, her mentor

And ... action!

Learning to be a good improv musician is a lot like learning to be a good actor. You get better by doing. You can read about and intellectualize improv all day long, but that only goes so far. There's only one way to really learn the art form: Take the leap and start playing. If you wait till you feel like you're perfect at it, you'll never do it at all.

The good news is, you don't have to know everything to get started. Just add your music little by little. Then allow yourself to expand as you get more comfortable.

One of the easiest ways to start is with a newer group that hasn't had a musician before. Then you'll all grow together. But even if you join an existing group, or replace or fill in for an established improv musician, you can do this.

Rehearse with the group, and try new games and genres. Above all, trust yourself and your instincts. And while you're at it, don't forget to have fun! Hopefully, that's why you're doing improv to begin with.

An Overview of Improv Comedy Formats

Improv has evolved a lot over the decades. Luckily, innovative groups continue to stretch the boundaries and experiment with new ways to present this spontaneous art form.

To help you get your bearings, here are some of the most basic formats you will encounter as an improv musician:

- Short form
- Long form
- Theme-based
- Improvised musical
- Stylized musical

Let's take a quick look at each one.

Short form

As the name implies, a short-form improv show features a series of brief performance pieces. Scenes usually last no more than a few to several minutes each. The host gets a new suggestion from the audience at the beginning of every new scene – and sometimes in the middle of a scene too.

Whose Line Is It Anyway? is a perfect example of short-form improv. It's fast moving and designed to get maximum laughs. Plus, it involves repeated input from the audience throughout the course of a show.

Short-form performance pieces generally fall into one of three categories:

- Games
- Scenes
- Songs

Games include things like Scenes from a Hat (where the players do quick one-liners inspired by an audience suggestion) or Doctor Know-It-All (where three players speak as one person by contributing one word each to answer audience questions).

Orchestrated Rant is another fun game where players expound on an audience-suggested topic whenever a director points at them. Bob created a game called Limerick All-Stars that has five players each supplying the line of a limerick on a topic suggested by the audience.

Scenes are different in that they involve characters, relationships, dialogue, and location settings. With scenes the improv players create a mini play on the spot.

Examples that fall into the scene category include Alphabet (where the first line spoken by each player must start with the next letter of the alphabet) and Film, Theater and TV Styles (where players must switch gears and continue a scene in a new genre style supplied by the audience).

Other scene examples include Sit, Stand, Lie Down (where three players must improvise a scene while being in different physical positions) and Hollywood Director (where three players must redo scenes based on a new style determined by the audience and a director).

A subcategory worth mentioning here is something called **Naive Games**. These games involve sending one player out of the room (or making sure they can't hear) and then getting suggestions from the audience on the identity of someone or something pertinent to the scene. The player is then brought back in to act out the scene as other players give them clues. By the end of the scene the "naive" player must guess the identity of the person or item.

Some popular examples in this category include Party Quirks, Dating Game, Debate, and Shopkeeper.

Songs are obviously music-based games. Some popular examples from *Whose Line* include "Irish Drinking Song" and "Hoedown." Greatest Hits is another crowd favorite (which has two actors playing the role of announcers who promote a new album while other players improvise songs based on the album theme).

We'll cover this song category in much greater detail in upcoming chapters.

Many short-form improv shows (like *Whose Line* and ComedySportz) are set up as pseudo, tongue-in-cheek competitions. Points are awarded to competing players or teams. Sometimes the players represent members of the audience, who win a prize if their player or team wins.

Other short-form shows, like Bob's Improv Comedy Cabaret, are presented as a noncompetitive variety show.

Long form

As you might have guessed, long-form improv shows do not consist of short, unrelated games and scenes. Typically, a single-word suggestion is obtained from the audience at the beginning, followed by a performance piece that lasts anywhere from 15 to 45 minutes or more.

There are as many types of long form as there are groups performing it. For our purposes here, we'll highlight two of the most popular:

- Harold
- Armondo

Let's examine each one ...

Harold

This form was created by improv legend Del Close and is popular at many improv theaters, including iO and the Upright Citizen's Brigade. Charna Halpern is credited with helping Del develop the form.

A Harold is based on what Del described as a 3x3 structure, but he encouraged groups to adapt the format, and many variations have been created over the years.

The basic 3x3 form consists of taking one suggestion from the audience, then the performance proceeds as follows:

- An opening group game that explores the theme. It can be short monologues, music, movement, or simple associations.

- Round 1: Three independent scenes, each based on some element of the theme.
- Group Game 1: Should be influenced by the theme but doesn't develop any of the previous scenes. It's sort of a palate cleanser.
- Round 2: Each of the three scenes develops further, raising the stakes and exploring links between the scenes and games.
- Group Game 2: Similar to Group Game 1.
- Round 3: Themes, characters, and games become connected. Scenes may merge together, some scenes might not be revisited. This is usually the shortest round, wrapping up all of the elements.

A musician can really help a Harold's structure, providing transitions and thematic underscore to help call back the different scenes. Some groups love to sing during a Harold if it happens organically in a scene; others don't. You have to be on your toes, because you never know.

Armondo

This format was created by Armando Diaz and has an even looser structure than a Harold. It also has many variations.

An Armando starts with a monologue by one of the improvisers, an audience member, or a celebrity guest. The monologue should be a true story from that person's life. Sometimes a suggestion is taken to inspire the monologue; sometimes not.

The actors then spin out scenes and games that are inspired by any element of the monologue they choose. The players don't simply recreate the story of the monologue; they take specific elements and create new scenes out of them. Sometimes the monologist tells a second story later in the show, but often not.

Again, a musician can help with transitions, calling back characters, improvising songs if the opportunity comes up, and generally supporting the players.

Theme-based

A popular trend in improv involves shows with a theme. They often tie into some well-known element of pop culture. Groups have done improv shows related to *The Twilight Zone*, *Gilligan's Island*, vampire movies, *Harry Potter*, *Star Wars*, and more.

Many groups do holiday and seasonal-themed shows: Christmas, Valentine's Day, Halloween, etc.

These themed shows can be produced using short form, long form, or a customized format based on the theme. Attaching a recognizable theme to a show can sometimes make it easier to market and set apart from more generic improv shows.

Improvised musical

Improvised musicals pull together all the elements of improv and musical improv, including dialog, songs, underscore, transitions, and choreography.

Some groups take one suggestion, such as a made-up title. Others take many suggestions and weave them together. Because improvised musicals tend to be longer structures – up to an hour or more – everyone in the cast gets to stretch and strut their stuff. The actors aren't as rushed with their characters and can develop them more. As for the music, it can be more thematic, with songs being reprised or reworked as underscore.

To pull this off effectively, all of the musicians and actors need to be well versed in musical theater conventions and familiar with the structure of classic musicals.

Stylized musical

Stylized musicals involve creating a complete musical as described in the previous section, but in the style of a specific era, genre or composer. Groups have done shows based on Stephen Sondheim, the golden age of musicals (like Rodgers and Hammerstein), operetta, Bollywood, *Glee*, etc.

Since this format goes so deep, the musician and actors need to be completely immersed in the style to be able to improvise a whole show based on it. However, if it's a style you already love, it can be a lot of fun to do the research and explore a particular musical style in a more in-depth way.

More improv formats

Improv is often used within the context of a scripted show and/or to create a scripted show.

For example, at The Second City, scenes created during the improv set are often turned into the written sketches that form the next review.

Many sketch comedy writers on shows like *Saturday Night Live* and *Key & Peele* come from improv backgrounds.

At theaters like The Annoyance in Chicago, improv is used to write new plays and musicals, and there will often be improvised sections within those scripted shows.

With a format called Playback theatre, performances are created by a team of actors, an emcee (called the conductor), and a musician. Audience members respond to questions from the conductor, then watch as the actors and musician create brief theatre pieces on the spot.

Another well-known format is murder mystery dinner theater, which usually relies on a mixture of scripted material and improv.

There are way too many improv formats and offshoots to list here. But this gives you a solid overview of the types of forms you may be called upon to support as a musician.

Section 2

The Heart and Soul
of Musical Improv

If this book was a Mexican restaurant, this section would be the Big Enchilada. In it Laura distills the core principles she has embodied over decades of performing musical improv.

You'll get a close-up look at the three fundamental aspects of supporting an improv show with music: transitions, underscoring, and improvising songs. You'll learn how to start, play and end songs, as well as how to perform a variety of styles to support your players and singers.

Get ready to learn and take lots of notes!

Transitions: How to Flow In and Out of Scenes and Tie Everything Together

One of the most important roles music plays in an improv show is creating smooth beginnings, endings and transitions. From starting the show and playing between scenes to ending with a bang, music helps make the show feel polished and connected.

Send in the crowds

Let's start at the beginning. All of the pre-show preparations have been made. The cast and crew are ready, the stage is set, and the house doors open. Now what?

It's really important to have some sort of house music playing as the audience enters and gets settled. Entering a quiet room can make people feel subdued and quiet, which is not good for improv. So fill the room with music that will amp up the energy and sense of fun.

You can use recorded music and a playlist you select ahead of time. You can play live or do a combination of live and recorded music. The main goal before the show starts is to create a fertile atmosphere for laughter to take root.

Starting the show

Whether you play beforehand or not, you need to have a pre-determined cue that alerts everyone involved that the show is about to start. A stage manager can cue you, a lighting change can let you know, the house music can fade, or someone can do an intro using an offstage mic.

Whatever method you use, you should discuss it with the cast and crew (and even do a dry run-through) beforehand.

You also need to be clear about who comes out first and how the show opening is structured. You don't want to bumble around or be uncertain in those first few moments. It can make the audience uneasy, which is hard to recover from.

Usually one of the actors will come out first to welcome everyone and explain the format of the show to the audience, whether it's long or short form. This person (who may or may not play the role of host throughout the night) will let the audience know that their participation is important. He or she might even have the audience practice giving suggestions.

The musician often goes out with the host at the beginning to get themselves situated. Or the musician can come out after the host's intro to play the rest of the actors onstage.

Sometimes groups use a CD or track to bring out the actors, but ideally the musician should play them on live. If you want to use a sequenced track, play along with it. This is a "live" improv show after all, so music in real time is an important part of it.

When you play the actors on, this is your chance to cut loose. You get to play loud, rock out, and even show off a little. Your music, the applause, and the actors running out should kick off the whole show in a fun, energetic way. It lets the audience know they're in for a good time.

Smooth transitions

Once the show gets rolling along you have more important work to do. Whether you're doing long or short form, your music serves as the glue that holds the show together when you play during the transitions between scenes. On *Whose Line*, Laura rarely plays transitions, but in a live improv show they are absolutely essential.

Music serves to wrap up one scene and lead the audience and players to the next. It gives the actors time to reset without dead air. It keeps the ball moving and the energy flowing. And, if a scene didn't go so well (which happens to the best of us), music can help bring the energy back up for the next one.

Ideally, there's a supportive rhythm as a scene or game ends. The actors wrap up the story, someone delivers a strong final line, and then laughter, applause and music all come together like a wave. It's exciting to ride that wave. In fact, that's why we do improv in the first place – to feel the adrenaline rush of a funny and well-performed scene.

Again, the music you play can be louder and busier right after a scene ends, because no one is talking or singing over it. Transition music doesn't have to be frenetic, but it should be energizing.

Short-form transitions

In short form, the transition music functions like a quick commercial break. This helps connect the various games and scenes, since they are rarely related to each other.

You can even end a scene with a musical joke. For instance, if the scene that just ended made a reference to *Star Wars*, you could play that theme music. We'll discuss this more in the upcoming section on underscoring.

Immediately following the transition music will be the setup for the next game. This will be delivered by either the host, as is done on *Whose Line*, or one of the actors, which is more common in live shows.

As the applause from the last scene fades, check to see if whoever is introducing the next game is in place and ready to go. Once they are ready, you should finish up what you're playing, even if it's at an odd place in the music.

You want to get to the next game intro quickly, so it's okay to leave the music "hanging" by not resolving or coming to a big finish. At this point you can either stop playing or play very lightly behind the actor who is setting up the next scene.

For example, the host or actor might explain, "Susan and Jim are going to play the Alphabet Game, where they take turns starting each line of the scene with the next letter of the alphabet."

The host will then ask for the suggestion of a letter, then something like a location, relationship, life event, etc. Once they have the needed suggestions, they'll say something like, "And now we take you to a park bench for the Alphabet Game, starting with the letter J."

Now you should play another transition into the scene, raising the volume briefly as the actors assume their characters. This music morphs quickly into underscore as you help establish or enhance the tone and rhythm of the scene that unfolds before you onstage.

Laura on audience volunteer games ...

In some games, like Sound Effects or Moving Bodies, not only is there an introduction, but someone also has to go get audience members to bring onstage. I like to play lightly under that activity. It helps the audience members relax a bit and not feel so rushed about getting to the stage. It also keeps that part of the show from feeling like dead air.

How do you know when a game is over?

On *Whose Line*, the host always calls the games out with a buzzer. But in live shows, any number of things can indicate an ending: music, lights (such as a blackout), an actor (often yelling "And scene"), or a combination of these elements can bring a game to a close.

With some short-form games, the end will be obvious. In the previously mentioned Alphabet Game, when the actors get to the last letter, the game is over. In Party Quirks, when the party host guesses all the quirks, the game is over. In Three-Headed Broadway Star, when the song ends, the game is over.

But with some games (like Film Noir, Living Scenery, and even Freeze Tag) the ending is not so obvious. Because they're more theatrical in nature, they have to wrap up in some way. Even for experienced improvisers, this can be a challenge. So you'll have to be extra alert and ready to help your players, if you can.

Music can definitely help a scene find its end. Underscoring can build to help drive a scene to an ending, and then that music can just continue through the transition. Laura likes to use a volume pedal with her keyboard so she can go seamlessly from quieter underscore to louder transition.

If you haven't been underscoring during most of the scene, starting to play can help guide your players toward an ending. You have to be subtle about it, though. You can't force a scene to end just by playing under it. But you can gently nudge it to a conclusion. (The great Fred Kaz was a master at this.)

If you're doing a game like Hollywood Director or Four Square, and you have a cast that likes to sing, some underscoring toward the end could lead nicely into a song, so be on your toes. Ending a scene with a song when it's not expected is like having a secret weapon.

Long-form transitions

Transitions tend to be more subtle with long form. They aren't used as "commercials" between separate, self-contained games. The music functions more like heightened underscore. Think along the lines of the transitional music you hear between scenes in films and musicals.

In a Harold, scenes usually end with a "wipe," where one of the actors crosses downstage to end one scene and start the next. If you aren't already playing, play along with the wipe and into the next scene. But there won't be a spoken intro into the next segment as with short form. The scene will just start.

If you're improvising a musical, most scenes end with a song. But even after a big finish, you'll often take a beat, then start a transition into the next scene under the applause.

In long form, without the structure of a host hitting a buzzer or calling scenes out, you may be relied on a lot more to help shape scenes and lead them to an ending.

Intermission

If you're doing a show that's longer than an hour or so, you'd be wise to schedule an intermission at the halfway point. If you're performing at a nightclub or bar, the venue will want you to take a break so they can sell more food and drinks.

Typically, after the last scene of the first act, the host or an actor will tell the audience it's time for intermission. At this point, one of two things can happen: you'll end the first act with a short flourish of high-energy music or some pre-recorded house music will come right on. Make sure you know which is going to happen ahead of time.

Then don't disappear. Check in with your cast backstage in case there are any changes in the second act, sound issues to be addressed, etc.

And, just as you did for the beginning of the show, clarify what your cue will be to start the second act. Open with some high-energy music, someone will introduce the first scene, and you'll be off and running again.

Ending the show

The end of the show is similar to the beginning. When the last scene or game ends, play like you did at the opening – loud and energetically – while the actors take their bows and the audience applauds wildly. Laura often plays the same music for the opening and closing, like a theme song.

In a short-form show, you'll usually know what the last game will be ahead of time. The director (or whoever is organizing the show) should have provided you and the cast with a set list, often called a running order or R.O.

But in long form, it's harder to know when a show should end. So be on your toes. If you're doing a Harold, Armando or an improvised musical, there can be a lot of threads to tie up. When things feel like they're wrapping up, and someone gets a strong laugh, it may be the perfect moment to end the show, so be ready.

The more you do long form, the more you'll learn your group's preferences and hone your instincts for when the end is near.

Again, you'll be riding a wave of laughter, applause and music as you bring the final scene and the show to a close. But what happens next? This is another logistical part you and your cast will have to work out.

Does everyone introduce themselves at the end? If so, are you playing under it (but more quietly, of course, so their names can be heard)?

They should also give a shout out to any sound or lighting people. Most importantly, when do they introduce and give props to you, the musician?

After that, what happens? Do all of the cast members run offstage and you're done? Or does someone make a closing announcement, plug the next show, remind the audience to tip the servers, etc?

As you can tell, there are a lot of details to work out with a live improv show. So, plan all these things out ahead of time so the end feels as smooth as the beginning. In fact, there's a show biz axiom that if you start strong and end strong, everything in the middle is gravy. In our experience, there's definitely truth to that.

As soon as the show is officially over, it's great to have recorded music start up. Your audience will be excited and eager to talk about the awesome show they just saw. If it's suddenly quiet in the room, you'll lose that energy.

After the show

If there's another group on the stage after you, and you brought your gear, be courteous and pack it up immediately after the show. Don't wander off, start talking to people, and leave the next group to work around your stuff – or worse, make them move your gear for you. Be professional. Also, clean up any mess you may have made backstage, especially if you share the space with other groups.

Do your best to personally thank the staff, tech people, and especially the sound person, if you have one (they can literally make or break a show).

What if the performance didn't go as well as you all hoped it would? Be kind and gracious with each other. No finger pointing or blaming is necessary. If there are issues to be worked out, do it at your next rehearsal, not backstage after the show.

Then go out and greet your adoring public. If they say they liked something, even if you weren't happy with it, don't tell them all the things that went wrong. Just say these two magic words: "Thank you." And consider adding something along the lines of, "I'm glad you enjoyed the show. Thanks so much for coming." Keep it simple and upbeat.

Here's another show biz nugget of wisdom worth mentioning: Even if the show tanked, never apologize for it. Expressing your appreciation is a much better way to go.

Underscoring: The Subliminal Art of Supporting an Improv Show

Underscoring in improv functions much like a film score in a movie or background music in a television comedy or drama. The music is almost subliminal in that it's best when the listener is barely aware of it. Yet it can be powerful in shaping the mood of a scene.

Laura rarely gets to underscore games on *Whose Line* because of the way the show is edited, but it's one of her favorite parts of playing a live improv show.

Underscoring can help establish a number of factors in a scene, including:

- The location: French cafe, church, swanky restaurant
- The time period: the Middle Ages, the Roaring Twenties, Ancient Greece
- The underlying rhythmic feel of a scene: frenetic, calm, monotonous
- A character's emotions: in love, frightened, angry

It can foreshadow what's to come, like in a horror movie, or help establish a flashback to the past.

Underscoring is one of the most powerful ways you, as the musician, can shape a show, even though the audience is usually not aware of it.

That means, to be effective you must avoid overplaying, either too loudly or too much. In this context, the musician almost becomes a stealth improviser.

Remember that silence can be just as powerful as music, so don't be afraid to lay low on some games and scenes. If you play through everything, the impact of underscoring will lose its power.

If you play into a scene, but don't want to continue underscoring throughout, it's usually better to fade out subtly, rather than resolving the music. This subliminally tells the audience that the scene is going to continue on without you. Experiment with ending in a way that leaves the music hanging. Try using a 4 chord, minor 6 chord, or suspended 5 chord. (We'll cover more on this chord numbering system in an upcoming section.)

Choosing when to play and when not to is another intuitive instinct you will develop as you do more rehearsals and shows. It will come easier as you get to know your cast. You will also develop your own style and sensibilities, which is one of the many joys of improv. So use your ears and trust your intuition.

Take note of what kinds of scenes come up often, and work on creating your own library of styles and feels to go with them. You'll want to have them ready to go so you can pull them up at a moment's notice, while also being ready to adapt them to the scene at hand on the fly.

Here are some go-to underscore styles Laura suggests you have in your musical back pocket. These will get you started, but you'll want to build your own library of styles.

- Film noir
- Childlike/playful
- Love scene/romantic
- Sad/melancholy
- Busy/frantic
- Sexy/sensuous
- Generic restaurant or elevator music
- Eerie/horror
- Office/business
- Patriotic

Bob on learning how to underscore in church ...

The first time I really grasped the power of underscoring was when I started playing Sunday services at spiritual centers (after years of playing in bars and nightclubs). When you perform at churches you generally have a more captive and focused audience, which allows you to do more subtle things vocally and musically.

I quickly learned to play softly behind guided meditations and provide a background musical bed when someone was speaking. For instance, if I performed with a singer, and she told a story before starting a song, I found that it sounded better if I gently played chords from the song behind her. When the story was over, I seamlessly went into the official start of the song. It created a nice sonic flow.

Believe me, these skills came in very handy as I added more music to my improv activities.

Using pop culture references

One of the fun things improv musicians can do is pull from their own basket of musical associations.

If a scene is set in a doctor's office, you might play a snippet of "Bad Case of Loving You (Doctor, Doctor)" by Robert Palmer. If the location is a church, you could play "Take Me to Church" by Hozier, "Son of a Preacher Man" by Dusty Springfield, or any traditional hymn. It's completely up to you and your musical point of reference.

You can add these types of snippets almost anywhere in a scene, but you'll find they usually work best at the beginning or the end.

Again, take time to create your own library of underscore sounds. Whether you've got "That's Amore" for an Italian restaurant, or "Somebody That I Used to Know" for a breakup scene, or the Jaws theme song for a scary moment, it will all come in handy at some point.

If you choose to add a musical joke like this, it works best if you get to it quickly and go right to the recognizable hook. Even then, the audience might not get it, or maybe only one or two people will.

Still, it will be good for you to take chances and make some bold choices (as long as you're not overbearing with the frequency). Like all improv, sometimes you'll fall flat and other times you'll hit a home run.

Taking underscore to the next level

An even more sophisticated way to play an associated song is to alter it to fit the tone of the scene. For example, for a Shakespearean style scene about a bad relationship, you could play "Hotel California" by the Eagles, but stylize it to sound like Bach. (Try it, it's pretty fun.)

In a dark, sci-fi style scene that takes place on the moon, you could play "Bad Moon Rising" by Creedence Clearwater Revival but in a dissonant, deconstructed way. You could do something equally creative with "Talking to the Moon" by Bruno Mars, "Walking on the Moon" by The Police, or "Moondance" by Van Morrison. (There is apparently no shortage of moon-themed songs.)

Feel free to deconstruct and rework any song to suit your needs. For example, try a slow, minor key version of "Take Me Out to the Ballgame" for a scene where the team is losing. A bluesy take on "Jingle Bells" works great for a swinging Christmas party.

If you want to get super creepy, play a children's song like "Rock-a-Bye Baby" in a high register with the chords in one key and the melody a half step down. (For example, chords in F, melody in E.) Fred Kaz was the master of this very effective trick.

Altering well-known songs like this can be rather subtle but intriguing to play. If nothing else, you might make one of the actors laugh.

Another choice you can make is to intentionally play against the expected tone of a scene. For example, if the suggestion is a funeral home, you might immediately start playing a bright version of "We're in the Money."

This musical choice would set the tone to be anything but somber. It could easily become a scene about characters who are comically fighting over money in the will.

To clarify, these references to popular songs should be played as instrumental underscore, not as songs the actors sing. You generally want to avoid doing parodies that are sung. But instrumental joke references are fair game.

Using Sound Effects

If you have the sounds available on a keyboard, and you know the group well, you can occasionally insert a sound effect into a scene. Adding thunder, a gunshot, or a phone or doorbell ringing, can bring a new element into a scene and challenge the actors to take it into new territory. Sometimes it can even help them get unstuck if they're struggling.

These kinds of strong offers require some real trust with your cast. It will help if you feel confident they'll receive the offer you make and run with it. You don't want to make an unexpected choice every time, but it can be fun once in a while to mix things up, especially if you play with a group often.

Laura on faking it ...

Here's a trick I use if I have only a vague idea of how to play a song I want to reference (and I figure I can fake it once I get going): I play it in whatever key I just played. For some reason this helps my ears latch onto it more quickly.

This trick also works when your singers start a song a cappella and you want to figure out what key they're in. Vocalists will usually sing in whatever key you played last. (This will especially come in handy if you don't have perfect pitch, which I don't).

Variety vs. continuity

When you provide underscore for an entire improv show, whether it's long or short form, it's best to play in a variety of styles, feels, major and minor keys, tempos, etc. You want to vary the mood throughout to keep things interesting.

If you're playing a long-form show, like a Harold or an improvised musical, you can take a more thematic approach. If, for example, in the first go around of a Harold you play something jazzy for a scene about a gambler in Las Vegas, when that character comes back later, by all means return to that jazzy musical theme. It helps the audience know that you've gone back to something that was established before.

Doing this gives the show continuity and shape. Then that basic theme you've created can grow and change with the character. If the gambler later gets dumped by the waitress at the casino, let the musical theme reflect his sadness.

Think about how in TV shows and movies the background music changes to reinforce the tone of different situations. In the same way, you can musically "track" a character, support their journey, and heighten their story arc.

A great game to help you and your cast connect through underscore is Emotional Soundtrack. Begin by playing any kind of music you choose. The actors then start a scene based on whatever your musical offer inspires.

Keep playing as the scene progresses, then change the underscore in mood, emotion, tempo, or feel and have the actors follow the musical change. Then change it again, as many times as it feels right. Your changes can be subtle or drastic, it's up to you. This game is often played without words, which can make it even more interesting.

Laura on being an underscored server at The Second City ...

When I was a waitress at The Second City, we would turn the theater over between shows – clear the dirty dishes, wipe the tables, reset the chairs, etc. There would be about eight of us bustling in and out of the room.

One night Fred Kaz was noodling at the piano while we worked, and I suddenly realized he was playing our entrances and exits. He had a different theme for each of us, and as we came in and out he would weave those themes together.

It was sort of jazz, sort of Bach. It struck me as being musical improv in its purest form; playing the rhythm of the room, the energy of the different "characters" coming and going, and doing it all just for its own pleasure. Brilliant!

Laura with (left to right) Susan Messing, Tom Booker,
and Ellen Stoneking from The Annoyance Theatre

With Roger Daltrey, who worked with Laura on a series of videos for kids

Improvising Songs: Three Types of Improv Song Structures

Let's get into the nitty-gritty of improvised songs and the various structures you can use to perform them. When it comes right down to it, there are basically three types of songs you will accompany your improv vocalists on. They are:

- Structured songs
- Semi-structured songs
- Organic songs

Let's take a closer look at each one.

Structured songs

Examples of games in the structured song category include *Whose Line* standards such as "Hoedown" and "Irish Drinking Song." (Google them if you're not familiar with the names.)

Structured songs are presentational rather than scenic. The actors usually stand in a line singing, rather than moving and interacting within a location. These songs have a strong emphasis on rhyming, and they tend to be joke-driven rather than character-driven.

With structured musical games, the chord progression, rhyme scheme, and often the vocal melody line are pre-determined. The singers know when to start and stop. As long as they're familiar with the structure, all they have to do is focus on the improvised lyrics and rhymes they come up with in the moment. Everything else is set. That makes structured songs popular with music directors and singers when they start out.

As the accompanying musician, the only time you'll actually improvise during a structured song is if you need to vamp between verses. This usually happens because a singer is trying to gather his or her thoughts or holding for the laughs created by the previous verse. Or sometimes a singer will get lost in the form, and you'll have to keep playing the chords until they pick it back up.

Semi-structured songs

Semi-structured songs (not surprisingly) fall somewhere between structured and organic songs. Unlike structured songs, the chord progressions, melodies and arrangements are not pre-set. Some of the games are presentational, with singers standing in a row (like Three-Headed Broadway Star and Conducted Song).

Other song games are more scenic but feature a "caller." The caller tells the actors when to sing, what style to sing in, and often what they'll sing about. But the musician gets to choose what to play within those parameters. Examples in this category are Scene to Rap, That Sounds Like a Song (aka Sing It), and Greatest Hits.

You may have seen Greatest Hits on *Whose Line*. Prior to starting the game, the host will ask the audience for an occupation or some other concept.

Let's say the chosen topic is "accountant." When the game begins, two players act like announcers during a TV commercial (played by Colin and Ryan on the show). They promote a new music collection called "Songs of the Accountant."

After some witty banter, each announcer highlights their favorite song from the album. Based on the audience suggestion, they make up a name for the song along with a genre, such as "I'll never forget that reggae classic, 'Keep Your Hands Off My Big Deduction.'" With that, the musician jumps into a reggae rhythm and the singer starts making up lines related to accountants and deductions.

Here's a tip: Teach your announcers to set up the style first, then banter a bit before they restate the style with the title. This gives you a little time to pull up a drum machine groove, keyboard patch, or guitar tone if you need it.

With a song game like this, try to keep the songs shorter, since there will be three or four of them on the same subject. When done well, this game is a real crowd-pleaser.

Another thing you can do with Greatest Hits is have the announcers name a popular artist instead of a generic genre: "My favorite is that Stevie Wonder song, 'I Love You Like a 1040 Long Form.'" Or, you can do an unlikely duet: "This amazing collection also features Bob Dylan and Pavarotti singing 'I Bet You Can't Claim This Exemption.'"

Of course, when you get this specific, it helps if you can mimic the style (more on this in the upcoming genres chapter) and your singers can do decent impressions of the chosen artists.

Laura on Greatest Hits ...

When we record Whose Line, *at the start of the week the producers give Linda Taylor and me anywhere from 25 to 75 song styles to prepare for Greatest Hits. (Yes, that's a lot!) We do research, sketch out chord progressions, find drum machine patterns, and decide on instrumentation.*

We work with the singers on some of them, especially if the styles are obscure or they are being asked to do an impersonation of a specific artist. But on the night we record, the singers don't know which styles will be used until Colin and Ryan say it in their live setups. And, of course, none of us knows what the subject of the album or song titles will be until we perform it live, based on a suggestion from the audience.

You can take this same approach if you do Greatest Hits in your live shows. However, no matter how familiar you are with the song structure, you'll need to be flexible as you both lead and follow the singers.

Another fun thing you can do with this game is be less structured and have the announcers surprise you with both the genre and title. To pull this off, you'll need to have a wide range of styles you can play at a moment's notice. And you'll need to know how to quickly use your keyboard or instrument to get the sound you want.

It will also help if the announcers know your range and abilities. And your singers will need to be confident enough to sing over whatever chord progression, groove or style you throw at them.

Sing It!

Another fun game in the semi-structured category is That Sounds Like a Song, commonly called Sing It. This is a scene-based game where two or more actors are given a suggestion and begin acting out a scene without music.

At various points an offstage caller will stop the action and have the players sing their lines for a short while, before returning to normal dialogue. Think of it as a short musical or an episode of *Glee*, where the characters periodically break into song.

With Sing It, the caller simply yells "Sing it!" when they want the actors to sing. With That Sounds Like a Song, the caller yells "Freeze," repeats the line of dialogue that prompted the stop, and has the audience shout "That Sounds Like a Song."

The musician starts playing whatever feels appropriate to the scene, and the actor who delivered the line now has to sing. As is the case with most improv games, there are many variations, regional differences, and ways you can play this one.

Organic songs

What Laura likes to call "organic songs" are truly created in the moment, with little or no planning ahead of time. You'll engage in this type of song especially when doing improvised musicals or long-form games such as a Harold.

However, there may be times in any game or scene when an actor might feel inspired to sing, or when another player challenges their stage partner to sing something.

Organic songs are scenic rather than presentational. They're more like songs you'd hear in a musical, and they are far less dependent on rhyming or jokes. The actors sing as characters within a location, often interacting with other characters while moving and/or dancing to heighten what they're singing. The best organic songs give insight into a character's emotions, wants, or point of view.

With this type of song, there's no predetermined pattern of who sings when or what the rhyme scheme is. They are open for other cast members to join in as needed, even if the song starts with a solo singer.

Organic songs have no pre-set chord progression, style, structure, or vocal melody that you have to follow. The songs can be short or long. The musician gets to choose what to play, based on the characters involved and the context and rhythm of the scene. You can pick whatever style, tempo or mood feels right to you.

Because these songs can happen at any time within a scene, the musician needs to be ready to jump in when needed. Pay attention to when a scene becomes heightened emotionally. For example, we discover that two women are long lost twins. Or a son tells his dad he wants to run off to join the circus. These are natural places for a song to take place.

At heightened moments like this you can play a little underscore that's appropriate to the scene. Then watch the actors to see if they transition into a song. If they don't sing, it's no problem, because what you played still worked as underscore. If they do sing, it ideally happens seamlessly within the scene.

It's a subtle process to lead into a song this way, so work with your actors to get comfortable with it.

On one hand, because organic songs are so spontaneous and flexible, they can be very freeing and fun. On the other hand, they can be intimidating to less experienced singers and musicians, but well worth exploring.

Bartender is a game that falls in the cracks between the semi-structured and organic song categories. With this one, an actor plays the part of a bartender, while up to three other actors are bar patrons. The host gets suggestions from the audience that each player uses to come up with a problem they are dealing with.

Example: A suggestion such as "picnic" might inspire a character who is afraid of ants.

One by one, each patron walks in and has some dialogue with the bartender. After a couple of spoken lines, the musician starts playing and the actor then sings about their dilemma.

While you can have familiar chords and styles that you plan ahead of time, this game works best when you simply choose something in the moment, based on what you intuitively feel the situation calls for. Once the actor playing the patron finishes their verses, the bartender sings a few lines in response. Your job as the musician is to listen, follow along, and support them.

Laura on "Hoedown" and song structures ...

Even though I've played them many times over the years, I have nothing against structured songs. (After all, playing "Hoedown" repeatedly helped put my kids through college.) However, playing the less structured songs is where you really get to stretch and improvise. So force yourself to move outside your comfort zone and venture into unstructured territory.

Be aware that some improvisers like singing to the more structured games, while others like the less-structured and organic games better. Eventually, you and your singers will want to get comfortable with all three types.

Laura performing with her husband, Rick Hall

The Fundamentals of Starting, Playing, and Ending Songs

Alright. We've gathered together all of our musical ingredients. Now let's cook up some songs. In this section we'll geek out on the mechanics of music.

Starting improv songs

As a musician who supports one or more improv singers, your first task is to play an introduction that immediately establishes the key and harmonic lay of the land.

Usually you'll define the tempo and rhythmic feel right away. Clarity is key when starting songs, since your singers have a lot to process at the beginning. You may be tempted to do your flashiest playing before they start singing, but it can make it harder for them to "get on the train" with you.

So keep things relatively simple and well-defined.

Another option ...

An alternate way to begin a song is to start out rubato (at a slower, looser tempo) and then later kick into the groove. This is common in styles like gospel and opera, as well as musical theatre and popular songs from the early to mid 1900s.

"Somewhere Over the Rainbow," for example, has a beautiful rubato intro, although it isn't always played. Ike and Tina Turner's "Proud Mary" is another popular example with a slower beginning verse.

A rubato intro can also organically occur in songs that grow out of underscore you play during a scene. Once a player starts singing – even if you've been meandering harmonically and rhythmically, which is fine for underscore – you'll need to settle into a tempo, key and chord structure.

A great time to kick into a new rhythmic feel is at the end of a singer's phrase, after they hold a note for dramatic effect. Practice this with your cast so you're all comfortable with it. When you use this technique in a show it will really impress the audience.

Bob on choosing chord patterns ...

When I support singers on an improvised song, I often use simple two- and four-chord patterns that repeat over and over. There are times when I'll go to a bridge, but I usually reserve those for veteran singers I have worked with who know how to handle the chord changes. Otherwise, the repeating four-chord structure is my personal staple.

There are all kinds of familiar chord pairings you can use. While there are plenty of interesting, jazz-inspired options, I feel that simple, meat-and-potatoes choices are the best way I can serve my singers.

The chord numbering system

Throughout this book we often refer to chords by numbers, using a simplified version of what's known as the Nashville Number System. The reason we use numbers (rather than chord names) is to help you understand the theory behind a chord progression and, most importantly, to help you play it in any key.

The numbers tell you the chords built on the scale degrees of any given key. For example, here are the scale degrees in the key of C:

Based on those scale degrees, we can build chords and number them accordingly:

You'll notice that some of the chords are major, some are minor, and one is diminished. The explanation of why that is goes beyond the scope of this book. Luckily there are plenty of online resources and books to learn more about chord theory and the Nashville Number System. (We have some recommendations in the Improv Resources section near the end of the book.)

Using this system, here's what a common doo-wop chord progression would look like:

1 – 6m – 4 – 5

In the key of C it would be: C – Am – F – G

In the key of F it would be: F – Dm – Bb – C

In the key of D it would be: D – Bm – G – A

Once you know the number system, you can quickly figure out any chord progression in any key.

Common chord progressions to use

The 1 – 5 – 6m – 4 chord pattern that the Australian band Axis of Awesome highlighted when they did a medley of 30 popular songs that use this exact chord progression. In the key of G, the chords would be G – D – Em – C.

The ubiquitous 1 – 4 – 5 chord pattern. It's the blues when played slowly and rockabilly when played fast. In the key of E you would play:

| E7 | | | |

| A7 | | E7 | | |

| B7 | A7 | E7 | B7 | |

Actually, any combination the 1, 4 and 5 chords in any key work well together. Just pick a tempo, feel and order for how the chords are played ... and repeat!

The descending pattern often associated with "Stray Cat Strut" by the Stray Cats: Bm – A – G – F#7.

Here's one that has been used a lot in guitar-based classic rock and folk songs: D – C – G – D.

Play around with simple tunes you already know, like campfire songs, jams you play at parties, songs you learned when you were a kid, anything easy. It's great training for your ear, and it helps you work with the chord numbering system and get comfortable with common chord progressions.

Here are a few easy ones:

"Louie Louie," "Twist and Shout" and "La Bamba":

| 1   4 | 5   4 |

"The Lion Sleeps Tonight":

| 1 | 4 | 1 | 5 |

"Knockin' on Heaven's Door" and "Helpless":

| 5 | 4 | 1 | |

You can take any song and deconstruct it. Strip away the melody and listen to it strictly as a chord progression. Slow it down or speed it up. Try substituting one or more chords with a related chord. For example, turn a 4 chord into a 2m or a 1 chord into a 6m.

Experiment with mashing up progressions from two different songs to create a fresh verse/chorus structure. Or use a different rhythm and see what happens. Try playing the chords to "The Lion Sleeps Tonight" but with a zydeco feel. Or play "Somewhere Over the Rainbow" as an R&B tune in 6/8 time.

As you play around with classic chord progressions, you'll leave the original song behind and create something that sounds both familiar and new. Just don't tell your actors what song you started with, or they'll have a hard time not singing the original melody.

Playing an improv song

Always remember, as the musician, you are the one who is primarily in charge of creating the overall song structure. The singers will be busy working on lyrics, rhymes, story and character choices. Therefore, it's your job to provide solid chord progressions and rhythmic support that are clear and easy to follow.

Unless you're doing something more freestyle like a mini opera or dream ballet, which can roam all over the place, you'll want to play some clear verse and chorus structures you can remember and repeat later in the song.

When you repeat a section of any given song, you can still adjust how you play it to the lyrics and characters at hand. For example, if you're doing a song about "The Three Bears," and each bear gets a verse, even though you'll play the same chord progression, you can give each verse a different feel. You could play it high and childlike for Baby Bear, bluesy and sexy for Mama Bear, and dark and dissonant for Papa Bear.

Ideally, an improvised song will come to a section the singers can repeat. This is called a chorus, refrain, hook, or tagline. That's where your skills in active listening come in. You'll need to pay attention to any phrases that your singers repeat and emphasize, and then follow their lead. You'll also need to remember the chords you played, so you can repeat them when you return to the chorus.

Even if you use the same chord progression for the verse and chorus of a song, you can create contrast by changing how you play it. To set off the chorus you might play more rhythmically, accent the downbeats, or play in a different register.

Encourage your singers to create contrast vocally as well. Have them experiment with singing different melodic lines for the verse and chorus, even if the chords stay the same.

For example, if the verse has quickly moving notes, they can hold out notes on the chorus. They can make the melody go up in pitch, or add harmonies, to help set the chorus apart from the verse. As with any good song, you want to find a balance between repetition and contrast.

The most common song structures you'll use

Sometimes the hook will be embedded in the verse. These types of tunes are called tagline songs. Examples include "The Lady Is a Tramp," "Great Balls of Fire," and "Saving All My Love for You." If you listen to any of these songs, you'll hear that the song title tagline comes at the end of each verse.

A popular tagline structure is:

Verse – Verse – Bridge – Verse – Repeat Tagline

Examples: "What a Wonderful World," "I'm on Fire" by Bruce Springsteen.

However, some tagline songs have the hook right at the beginning of each verse, as in "From a Distance," "Earth Angel," and "Angie." And every once in a while it's at both the beginning and the end, as in "Georgia on My Mind."

While many songs have a repeating tagline embedded in the verse, the most common hook is a stand-alone chorus, which features a chord pattern and melody line that's usually different from the verses.

To execute this structure when improvising, you and your singers will want to keep the chorus musically and lyrically simple. Why? Because you'll have to remember it so you can repeat it later. Plus, a lot of hit songs have super simple choruses. Consider "All About That Bass" by Megan Trainor and "Don't Stand So Close to Me" by the Police. Simple choruses also make it easier for more advanced singers to create harmonies and countermelodies on the spot.

Here's how a classic verse/chorus song is often structured:

Verse – Chorus – Verse – Chorus – Bridge – Repeat Chorus

Examples: "Ain't No Mountain High Enough," "Moves Like Jagger," "What Doesn't Kill You Makes You Stronger," "Take My Breath Away."

We've given you some classic forms, and they're classic because they work well. But remember, there are many variations in popular music, and even more so in musicals and improvised songs.

A lot of songs don't have a bridge at all ("Ho Hey" by the Lumineers,

"Killing Me Softly With His Song," made popular by Roberta Flack), while some have two bridges ("Happy" by Pharrell Williams). Sometimes a song will start with a chorus ("Let's Dance" by David Bowie, "Brass Monkey" by the Beastie Boys).

Many songs have a pre-chorus that comes after each verse (Taylor Swift's "We Are Never Ever Getting Back Together," Mumford & Sons' "I Will Wait"). Don't feel like you have to use complex structures like these, but don't be afraid of them either. If they happen naturally in the course of a song, don't try to force it back into a tidier form.

You can have ideal structures like these in mind when you start a song, and do your best to lead your singers to them. However, it often won't work out that way.

You might have a great four-bar turnaround, but your singer comes in after two and a half bars. Even though it's not what you had in mind, you are now at the beginning of the next section. Or a singer might vocalize a melodic idea that doesn't go with the chord progression you started, so you will have to adjust.

A big laugh, dance break, or another actor entering the scene can also derail the best laid song structure plans. That's when vamping comes in handy. Often times, you can simply hang on the 1 chord. For example, if you're playing a four-chord doo-wop pattern in the key of A, you can just vamp on A until the singer is ready. Or you can help lead them in by playing a strong 5 chord (in this case, E7), with bass line movement that walks back up to the A.

Remind the singers that it's like jump rope. The musician can keep going around until they're ready to jump in.

Laura on being fluid and flexible with songs ...

Here are some examples of improvised songs I've been a part of that took an unexpected twist:

- *A character turned into a werewolf mid song, so I quickly transformed a Motown groove I had been playing into a dark, operatic feel.*
- *During a* Les Misérables-*style ballad, one of the characters dreamed of being a stripper, so the music I played morphed into a sultry blues vamp, then back to* Les Mis.
- *A song by an actor playing a nervous teen trying to ask a girl for a date jumped all over the place, rhythmically and structurally, which helped emphasize his awkwardness.*

Remember, none of these sudden changes are mistakes. In fact, often times this is where the most interesting improv happens. So don't get flustered or mad. Just hang on, listen to the offers the actors are making, and let yourself be part of the flow.

Ending an improv song

Ending together can be the hardest part. It's important to remember that the more people involved in a song (musicians and singers), the more challenging it will be. In a group number, the musician will probably have to lead the charge to get all of the players to end at the same time. But when it works, it looks and sounds like magic to the audience.

Luckily, when performing songs (unlike when acting out scenes) it's okay to cue each other on stage, so don't be afraid to.

In group numbers in particular, it's great if you have a strong singer who can take the initiative and help everyone wrap it up. They can even turn and conduct the other singers, give you a visual cue, or say something like "One more time!" or "Here we go!" Even in the middle of a song, a confident singer can shout out "To the bridge" to steer everyone into a new section. (Hey, it worked for James Brown).

The advantage of having one of the singers give cues is that they are on stage, so it's easier for the other singers to see and hear them. It can be harder for the musician(s) to cue, since we are typically on the side, but it's not impossible. If you want to be able to visually cue the actors, you have to train them to keep you in their peripheral vision, especially as a song is drawing to a close.

Speaking of visual cues, as you get used to working with the same actors and singers, you will slowly create an unspoken language with each other. Wayne Brady is really good at cueing Laura and Linda Taylor, not only to indicate the end of a song, but all throughout it.

A certain gesture might indicate the singer wants you to keep repeating the current chord progression. Another could signify they want to switch to the chorus or bridge, while a different motion can tell you they are ready to end the song.

You can either formalize these gestures with all of the singers in a group, or you can just watch their body language and learn how each singer naturally communicates with you.

A few things you can do musically to end songs

As you steer a song toward an ending, it's important to telegraph it to all of the singers (and other musicians, if you have them). You can lead to most endings with a good old 4 – 5 – 1 or 2 – 5 - 1 chord progression. (In the key of G this would be C – D7 – G or Am - D7 - G.) Strong bass movement that walks from the 5 chord to the 1 really helps let everyone know where you're going.

Whether a song is a solo, duet or group number, the easiest way to end is for everyone to come to a repeating tagline or chorus. After they've sung it a few times, you can ritard the tempo and do a slow, dramatic version of the line to end the song. Of course, your singers need to pay attention and match the slower speed.

A powerful choice for a rhythmic up-tempo song is to end with an abrupt, hard stop at the end of the last line, which typically comes on the first beat of a measure. Just be careful with this ending and do your best to indicate to everyone that it's coming. You don't want one player to miss it and keep singing after everyone else has stopped.

Another option is often called a "trash can" ending where you hold out a final word or note with a big flourish.

And, in the same way you can start some songs rubato, you can end a song by having the singer emote a final line at a much slower tempo.

As is the case with all of the song structure examples, listening intently and being flexible is key.

An Overview of Styles and Genres You Can Use in Musical Improv

One of the questions Laura gets asked the most is, "How do you learn to play in so many different styles?"

If you've seen the most recent seasons of *Whose Line* on the CW Network, you may have noticed the music gets pretty deep into specific styles. One of the reasons is because the show used a lot of generic music categories in earlier seasons and the producers didn't want to keep repeating the same song styles.

So now, instead of doing reggae, they'll tend to go with a specific reggae artist, such as Bob Marley. Or they'll go into a subgenre like dance hall. Sometimes the genres get really obscure. Chinese opera, anyone? How about some Russian folk metal?

Luckily, in most improv shows you won't have to go so deep into these subgenres or specific artists. If you ask the audience for a suggestion of a musical style for a game like Greatest Hits, you'll probably get something broad like blues, country, musical theatre, etc. However, you will encounter "clever" attendees who will try to throw you a curve. So be ready.

Here's the thing: You don't have to ask the audience for musical styles if you don't want to, especially when you're starting out. You can pick the styles yourself or have whoever is calling the game pick them. Or, if you have a handful of styles you and your cast are comfortable with, you can write them on slips of paper or a dry-erase board and have an audience member pick one. As you and your group get comfortable with more styles, you can add them to the mix.

All of us have styles we're more familiar with and better at playing, which is a great starting point. But you'll also want to listen to and learn styles that are outside your comfort zone. You'll have to work to have something "in your hands" to cover most styles – chords and rhythms you can call up immediately.

Don't stress out about it

The good news is, you don't have to play obscure styles or feels precisely. You just need something that is immediately recognizable. You're mainly striving for a cliché or stereotype of the music category. (We know, this may make some serious musicians cringe. But that's part of your role as an improv musician.)

In a live improv show you have very little time to establish a style with the singers and the audience, so you want it to be clear right away. Luckily, you don't have to be completely authentic with a style for it to work. You only need to hint at it and then let the singers and audience do the rest.

If you're working with a group regularly, and there are styles they do often, you should have more than one way to play them. If you get the suggestion of Latin music a lot, work up several sub-genres. You could have a salsa, mariachi, bossa nova, etc. Be sure to play it in different keys, too. That way, when Latin gets called, you have choices, you can challenge your singers, and you can avoid the dreaded ruts.

And certainly, if you do a style-oriented show – like an improvised Bollywood musical, for example – then you can go really deep into the style and know it inside and out.

Laura on answering the style question ...

People often ask me, "How do you approach and learn a style you're not familiar with?"

I think of this as investigative research. It appeals to the part of my brain and soul that yearns to understand the structure of music. What makes a certain style tick? What sets it apart from other styles?

I love being a perpetual student. If you want to be a great improv comedy musician, develop your curiosity. Be eager to look under the hood and ask yourself, "What makes this musical style sound like this style?"

Learning a new style

The best way to get started is to do a lot of listening. YouTube, Spotify, and other streaming services are great resources for this. Find several artists in the genre you want to learn and listen to a handful of tracks.

Next, pick some songs that exemplify the genre and play along with them. Figure out the chord progressions by ear if you can (it's great ear training). If you need to, search for the chords online. Or, if you read music, you can see if sheet music is available. Whatever you do, play along with the tracks, because that's how you transfer the feel of the songs from your ears to your hands.

Now, pick one or two tracks that best represent the style and do some analysis. Here are elements to look for:

- What is happening rhythmically? (Laura feels this is the most important element of all.)
- What is the bass line doing rhythmically and harmonically?
- What accents are the drums hitting?
- How does the vocal move rhythmically relative to the accompaniment?

In addition, ask yourself:

- What kinds of chords are being used? Are they simple triads or more complex chords?
- What kinds of chord progressions do you find? Are they simple or complex?

Does the style use lots of open 5ths (heavy metal, hard rock, Gregorian chant, pirate)? Or mostly dominant 7ths (rock, country, blues, zydeco)? Or lots of major 7ths (bossa nova, R&B ballad, disco)? Or diminished, extended and other sophisticated chords (jazz, Sondheim, gospel)?

Look at the overall structure of the songs. Are they simple looping four- or eight-bar phrases (dance music, hip-hop, funk)? Or are they complex structures (musical theatre, pop ballad) or more free flowing (opera, rock opera, new age)?

What kinds of instruments are normally used to play this genre? And what do you have to work with? For example, if you have a synthesizer and you want to do bluegrass, a split with acoustic bass in the left hand and banjo in the right will serve you. If you have a guitar player, have them strum away on an acoustic.

What kinds of licks, riffs or fills are associated with this style? You don't have to master a ton of licks for each style; just enough to give a flavor.

Bob on the danger of doing song parodies ...

In this chapter we are examining how to analyze and mimic music styles. This type of thinking can lead some musicians to simply play the chords and structure of specific popular songs verbatim. In essence, they turn an opportunity to create a spontaneous original tune into a song parody.

Laura and I are in total agreement that, as a general rule, song parodies (a la "Weird Al" Yankovic) should be avoided, even when they're made up on the spot. Unless you're doing a song parody game or it comes up organically in a scene, please don't make playing parodies your go-to strategy.

I've seen seasoned improvisers use obvious karaoke tracks in shows. I've witnessed musicians who play nothing but recognizable chords from popular songs throughout an entire improv set.

You may think that playing the accompaniment to popular songs helps your singers, but I think it does a disservice to the audience by pulling them out of the moment as they try to recall why the song sounds familiar.

The ideal approach as an improv musician (and a singer, for that matter) is to capture the feel of a particular style or artist; not to copy it directly. Musically dance all around it, but make the song a unique composition that stands on its own.

How to analyze a musical style

Let's say you wanted to mimic the vibe of the late '90s "boy band" pop sound. This genre was most notably shaped by acts such as Backstreet Boys and NSYNC.

After listening to several songs in the genre, you choose NSYNC's "Bye Bye Bye" for a more in-depth analysis. Here are some of the musical details you might uncover:

- **Rhythm**: Syncopated, hip-hop based. Lots of hits and stops and rhythmic interest.
- **Chord progression**: Diatonic, minor key. The verse and chorus are similar harmonically. The chorus descends by whole steps.
- **Kinds of chords**: Simple triads.
- **Song structure**: Slow intro, then eight-bar phrases that loop. A pre-chorus sets up the chorus. The breakdown hangs on the 1 chord.
- **Instrumentation**: Drum machine, synth bass, synth pads, horns, and strings.
- **Licks**: Horn stabs, with arpeggios to set off the sections.
- **Singers**: Lots of harmonies. Great groove for dancing.

Encourage your actors to do their homework so they can master new styles too. Have them watch YouTube videos to work on vocal phrasing and tone, and maybe even learn some dance moves. Wayne Brady constantly studies musical styles, old and new. It's part of why he's so brilliant at what he does.

Your actors don't have to do impersonations of specific artists unless they want to. They can study artists just to get a general feel for a style. However, if a Morrissey impersonation helps them get into '80s pop, or doing Janis Joplin brings out their inner rock goddess, by all means encourage them to do it.

Laura on making song styles your own ...

Once you've analyzed a style, it's your chance to play around and come up with your own version. I often keep one part of the structure, then change some of the other elements. For example, I might keep the rhythmic accents but change the chord progression. Or, I might use a similar chord progression but alter it rhythmically.

If I get stuck on the original version of a particular song, I might pick another one in the genre and analyze it. Then I try to mash up the two, so what I end up playing doesn't sound like either song.

Be flexible, keep it simple

Your goal is to be familiar enough with a style to be able to create something new and original, without losing the authentic feel of the genre. But don't forget, you also need to be flexible and support what your singers do.

When you consider playing a particular style, think about what you could do for a verse, pre-chorus, chorus, bridge, and breakdown in that style. You probably won't get to all those sections, but it's comforting to know you'll be ready if the opportunity arises.

However, don't hesitate to keep things simple. Especially if you have inexperienced singers who might miss a pre-chorus, just skip that part.

The bottom line is to be prepared. That way, when you're in the middle of a live show, you can relax and have the confidence that you'll instinctively know what to do to support your fellow players and the scene.

Laura on the set of *Whose Line*, with Greg Proops, Wayne Brady, Colin Mochrie, and Ryan Stiles

An Improv Karaoke recording session (left to right): Keegan-Michael Key, Laura Hall, Rick Hall, and Ron West

Section 3

It's Show Time – Now What?

Now that you've been given the Holy Grail of musical improv (in the previous section), it's time to launch into your next show, right?

Not so fast!

To make sure you're completely ready, let's examine a few important things:

- what instrumentation and gear you'll need to bring
- where to set up on stage and position yourself for optimum impact
- how to warm up your singers and yourself

Sound good? Let's get cracking!

Instrumentation and Gear Options for Improv

So far in this book we've been using the generic term "musician" to refer to you or whoever will accompany your improv group. Of course, there are many types of musicians, instruments, and music gear options. We'll cover a range of them in this section – from the commonplace to the more unusual.

A "classic" improv musician (like Fred Kaz) could do an amazing show with just an acoustic piano and nothing else. If you're a pianist, even if you sometimes use a drum machine or keyboard, you should still be comfortable doing a show in its most stripped down form like this. It forces you to get back to the basics – no bells and whistles, just your connection to the actors and the game at hand.

That being said, there are so many different ways people play improv shows nowadays. And there are lots of production levels you can add to a live performance. It depends on the group, the show, the space you're in, etc.

If you're performing in a little comedy club, you might use just a piano or keyboard. If you're playing a big room in Vegas, you might want to add more instruments, players, gear and pizzazz.

Some groups that don't have a musician available use pre-recorded music, such as Laura's *Improv Karaoke* CDs. (How's that for a subtle plug?) While not as spontaneous as a live musician, using recorded music let's you add high-quality rhythm tracks that your singers can improvise over.

Other groups take a hybrid approach and combine recorded music or sequenced tracks with a live musician. For instance, they may use the recorded tracks for transitions and their musician for the improvised games. The only downside of this hybrid format is that the tracks can make those transitions seem separate from the rest of the show, too polished sounding for a show that is being made up on the spot.

Here's a good compromise: If you use sequenced music, leave some space to play along with the tracks during the show. This will add a live feel to the pre-programmed tracks.

Some improv groups use a guitar player or small band. Laura once saw a group that used a vibraphone player as their musician. Now that was different. Any instrumentation can work as long as you and your cast are all working together.

A band can be really fun, as long as you have time to rehearse and get in a groove together. One of you will need to be the musical director to make it work. That person will choose keys, count off songs, keep an eye on the actors, cue everyone when it's time to change sections, and help navigate the ending.

The more players you have, the more you need to listen to each other, because there's a greater chance of things getting muddled. *The key to success is active listening!*

It's the same way with singers: the more you have, the more everyone has to listen and tune into each other.

Laura on her gear setup ...

When I'm the only musician playing a bigger live improv show, I usually use a piano, synthesizer and drum machine. With that gear I can cover most styles. I also like to bring an inline volume pedal for the keyboard so I can easily move from underscoring into a song or scene transition without taking my hands off the keyboard to adjust the volume.

On Whose Line, *because it's television, we pull out all the stops. The multi-talented Linda Taylor joins me. Between the two of us, we usually have a piano, two synths, four drum machines, acoustic and electric guitars, bass, banjo, and ukulele. We can cover a lot of musical ground with all those tools at our disposal.*

More geeky stuff for the keyboard players: I like to have all of the synth patches and drum patterns that I use often ready to go and easy to access. I find myself regularly using patches such as piano, electric piano, organ, harpsichord, koto, accordion, and strings.

If you have a keyboard that has a split mode option, it's really handy. I set up splits with an electric or acoustic bass in the left hand and piano, organ, vibes, accordion, or horns in the right hand.

Drum patterns I use often include disco, 6/8 rock, shuffle, R&B ballad, reggae, hip-hop, gospel, etc. Some drum grooves can work for more than one genre. For example, a shuffle can be used for country, blues and rock. A disco feel also works for a lot of contemporary dance music. Figure out ahead of time what tempo is good for each style.

Get to know your gear and set it up in a way that makes sense to you. That way, when you're doing a show, the tech won't be distracting.

Banding together

It's a great idea to find out if anyone in your cast plays an instrument and would want to play during an improvised song. Almost any musical addition can work, but instruments like harmonica and percussion are especially easy to add into the mix.

Laura once coached a group in Chicago called Los Improviachis, in which all of the actors are also musicians. They take turns playing for each other. It's tricky sometimes for them to make the transition from actor to musician and back, but it's so much fun for the audience.

Bob on using the guitar as your main improv instrument ...

When I first started doing improv, the only instrument I'd ever witnessed used with a group was the piano. But I was a guitar player. So, without any improv guitar player examples to go by, I used what I had and figured it out as I went.

I admit that a keyboard/synthesizer is probably the most versatile instrument. If you can quickly switch between playing a piano, organ, string section, and dozens of other sounds, you've got a wide range of styles and feels covered.

However, I believe some things simply sound better on guitar. The jangly sound of folk, Americana and country songs sound right at home on an acoustic guitar. And on the rock side of things, nothing can beat an electric guitar with a little overdrive chunking along. Guitar is also great for rockabilly, funk, blues and jazz sounds.

And, if you use an effects pedal, you've got an even wider assortment of sounds at your fingertips. So, if you're a guitarist who wants to do improv, have no fear. I've been doing it for many years.

Adapting your instruments and gear to various styles

The gear and instrumentation you use can affect how realistically you cover different musical genres. For instance, it's a lot easier to play heavy metal with a drum machine and an electric guitar (although there is something funny about playing a classic Led Zeppelin-style song on the piano).

Of course, the instrumentation is not the only thing that determines a scene style or musical genre. As we discussed in Section 2, you should research genres and think about the rhythms and chord progressions that are characteristic to each one.

What makes reggae sound like reggae? Or Motown sound like Motown? It's partly the way it's sung, partly the instrumentation, but also the way it's played. So how you play, regardless of what instrument you use, will go a long way in getting your singers in the groove.

Laura on her biggest *Whose Line* gear malfunction ...

One of the things people remember the most about me from the ABC version of Whose Line *was, of course, the time something went horribly wrong. We were improvising a Village People-style song to an audience member named Howard. The first problem arose when Wayne called out the guy's name (a la "YMCA") and misspelled it H-O-R-W-A-R-D.*

Then, somehow, the drum pattern on my keyboard started speeding up. (This was after Wayne spelled the name wrong the first time, so at least I wasn't responsible for that!) I remember looking down at the keyboard, completely baffled by the increasing tempo.

I glanced up to see poor Colin trying to dance and sing faster and faster, until the whole song melted down and I had to just turn the keyboard off to get it to stop. When Drew asked me what had happened, I laughed so hard I was crying. I could barely speak. Plus, I really didn't know what had gone wrong.

Of course, the guys had to comment on it, which made it even harder for me to stop laughing. Colin said, "I don't think it was that noticeable." And in his classic style, Greg Proops added, "Watch out for those tempo changes, man ... 'cause when we go into the second bridge, this sh*t takes off!"

I figured out later there was a little button on the keyboard I'd never noticed before. It was marked "ACC," for accelerate. I must have accidentally bumped it while I played the song. You can bet I was careful not to touch that button again (although sometimes I threatened the cast that I would use it if they didn't behave).

What to Do Before the Show

Great! You've got a gig with an improv group. After you celebrate, what should you do to get ready for the big show? Let's start from the beginning.

If the show is at a venue where you've never performed, you'll want to find out a few quick things. For instance, do they have a piano or keyboard already in place? If it's an electronic keyboard, what brand and model is it? Are you familiar enough with it to use it? If you're not, make sure you arrive in time to get comfortable with it before the show.

When the venue provides a keyboard, Laura always brings her own sustain pedal, as it's often the piece that's missing. Get a pedal with a dual polarity switch, which generally works with all keyboards.

Most likely, especially if you play the guitar or some other instrument, you'll want to bring your own instrument. You'll also want to know if the venue has a sound system. Some do, some don't. If they do, can you plug into it? If they don't, can you bring an amplifier, if one is needed?

With most of his improv gigs, Bob simply plays an acoustic guitar with no amplification. It's not needed, since the actors in his group rarely have an opportunity to use microphones. (We'll cover more about mics in a minute.) Laura tends to play larger venues, where she prefers to bring her own gear and be amplified. Every show and venue will be different, so be prepared to be flexible.

Whenever you can, try to do a site visit of any new venue you play. If that's not possible, visit their website, email, or call to get as much information as you can in advance.

What to bring

If there's any chance your instrument will be amplified, you'll be wise to bring a quarter-inch cord, a direct box, and an XLR mic cord. These three items will provide just about everything you'll need to hook into an existing venue sound system.

If you use a wireless system for your guitar or other instrument, make sure you have all the components you need: transmitter, receiver, connector cords, and extra fresh batteries.

Will you play any pre-recorded music before, during or after your show? Then you'll want to bring the laptop, iPod, iPad, CD player, or whatever it is you play the music from, as well as any associated connectors.

Of course, if you supply your own microphones for the actors or for yourself, be sure to pack and take those. It wouldn't hurt to bring extra cords, guitar strings, and other related gadgets too.

Can you see me now?

Now that we've covered what gear to bring, let's address another important matter: the best place to position yourself so you have good sight lines and can clearly see the actors – without being too "out front." Usually, that ideal position is somewhere close to the action but off to the side.

If you're too far back (or up stage, away from the audience), you'll only be able to see the actors' backs, and that's not ideal. A good side view works best.

Why is this important? Having a good sight line will greatly help you stay connected to your actors. You can cue them visually, when needed, and they can cue you. This ideal placement will give you a front-row (or more accurately, a side-row) seat to the performance. It will allow you to get a feel for each scene, sometimes even before the actors say or sing a word. Their body language alone can direct and inspire you.

Can you hear me now?

Before the show starts (and preferably before audience members start to arrive) make sure you do a complete soundcheck to ensure that everything is good to go. Otherwise, it can be very distracting to work out audio issues during the first part of a show.

First and foremost, is your instrument working and can it be heard? If the venue has stage monitor speakers, can you hear yourself? How is the sound coming out of the main speakers that face the audience? Is it loud enough without being too loud? Can you hear the cast, and can the cast hear you?

It's vitally important to make sure everyone can hear. This applies to the cast, the musician, and the audience. If the actors do not use mics, the musician has to really be diligent about keeping the volume low enough so the audience can clearly hear the actors.

Whether you're underscoring a scene or supporting an improvised song, the actors have to be heard. During transitions is the time when you can play louder to help keep the energy flowing into the next scene or game.

If the audience can't make out the witty words an actor is emoting, all is lost. So please respect your role and responsibility in this delicate balancing act.

Singing to the back row

The actors also carry the responsibility of making sure they project their voices and are loud enough so everyone can hear them. An old theatre adage is to speak (and sing) at a volume that allows someone sitting in the very last row to hear you. Laura asks her actors to give her a simple hand signal (a quick thumbs up or down) if they need more or less keyboard volume. (They hardly ever need more!)

Many theaters will have a microphone or two that the actors can use for singing. Make sure the actors are comfortable with the mics. You can help by going over some basic mic technique with them. Improvisers tend to get too loud and close to the mic, which causes uncomfortable volume peaks and distortion.

Most mics have a sweet spot position between two and six inches away from a singer's mouth. An experienced performer will know to move the mic away when belting out a note and to move it closer when whispering or doing soft vocal parts. Encourage your singers to experiment with the mics beforehand to get accustomed to using them properly.

If you're in a larger or more professional venue, the actors may be able to wear wireless clip-on mics, known as lavaliere or lapel mics. You'll definitely want to do a soundcheck with these and warn your actors not to stand too close to the monitors or main speakers.

Lapel mics are notorious for feeding back, so ask your actors to move around the space to find out where the danger zones are. These mics should be run as low volume as possible in the monitors to help prevent feedback.

Some actors like to use a lapel mic for scenic work, but prefer a handheld mic for singing. It makes them feel like rock stars, lounge singers, or whatever. If you can, let them have that experience.

Pre-Show Warm-Up Exercises

A good improv actor knows the importance of warming up before a class or a show – especially a show. You never want to hit the stage cold. That's why you must prepare your mind, your body, and your mouth for a performance.

Pre-show warm-ups should include singing activities. These exercises will not only loosen up the players' singing voices; they will also warm up their sense of rhythm and rhyme.

Depending on the venue, you may be able to warm up onstage before the doors open. Or find a space backstage, outside, or in some other out-of-the-way place. Regardless of where you gather to warm up, be sure to make the time to do it before the show starts.

Improv warm-ups should be purposeful and fun. Feel free to create or adapt your own warm-up games, especially as you get to know the singers in your group.

For example, do you have a great soprano? Make sure you warm up into her upper register. Is singing together a challenge for your group? Do some rhythmic exercises. Does your cast struggle with staying in character when they sing? Have them sing in gibberish, so they're focused less on the lyrics and more on the character.

Here are some of our favorite musical warm-up games we've either learned, made up or adapted. Some of these activities go by various names, so you might already know them by a different name.

Choir of Angels

Good for: finding harmonies, following chord progressions, listening and blending, taking turns, switching from background vocalist to lead vocalist

Have your singers stand in a circle. Play a simple chord and have them all find a harmony note within the chord, singing "ooo." (For some of them this might be easy; for others a real challenge). Now play through an easy chord progression at a medium tempo. Something simple like a measure each of C – F – C – G – C – F – G7 – C.

Ask the players to move vocally as needed to harmonize with the changing chords. Instruct them to listen to each other and blend, just like a choir.

If this goes well, try another chord progression in a different key and make it a "line at a time" song. Get a topic suggestion and have them start ooo-ing in the background. Then go around the circle and have each player add a line to the song.

When they're ooo-ing, they have to be quiet enough to hear and follow the story. But when it's their turn to add a line to the story, they need to sing out. This warm-up is not intended to be a rhyming game; it's all about telling a cohesive story as a song.

Gibberish

Good for: singing in character, letting go of rhyming, tapping into the emotion of a song, not worrying about lyrics, hearing the form of the music

Play a simple 8- or 16-bar chord progression. One at a time, have each player sing through the form in gibberish, using whatever melody they choose to vocalize over your chords. The goal of this exercise is to communicate who they are, where they are, what they're doing, and their emotional state – all without words.

Each person should find their own melody, their own style of gibberish, and their own character. Honestly, gibberish songs can sometimes be more compelling than songs with words.

As the musician, this exercise is a good one for you to play in different ways to support each character. You'll use the same chord progression for each one in the group, but you can adjust how you play it for each character. If one player becomes a big, burly construction worker, you could play it more heavy handed. If the next character is a prim and proper librarian, adjust to that feel.

Gibberish is a great warm-up, but it can also be played as a game in a show.

Walk About

Good for: gently warming up the voice, listening, space awareness, staying together

Have your singers walk around the space, even backstage and into the audience, while vocalizing. Play softly and instruct them to sing quietly enough to hear you and each other.

Ask them to take notice of how different the sound can be in different parts of the room. This will make your players aware of the challenges of staying together rhythmically when they are spread apart and moving around.

Start playing a melody around middle C at a medium tempo. Ask them to join in. Move up and down the scale as they stretch their voices. Have them sing on different open syllables, such as moo, zee, so, ta, etc.

For fun, have the singers add characters or locations, while still singing along with the exercise ("You're all cavemen." "You're on a hike in the Alps.")

Here's an example of two simple melodies you can play for this exercise:

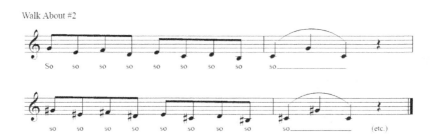

You don't need an instrument for the following exercises, so they're great for backstage or in a green room. Since you won't have to play, you can join the actors if you want.

Tongue Twisters

Good for: articulation, listening and following, staying in time together

One person leads the group through tongue twisters, with the rest of the group echoing. Encourage everyone to speak lightly and clearly, staying in time together. This game is about clarity, not volume.

Recite classics like "Rubber baby buggy bumpers" or "She sells sea shells by the sea shore." You can find plenty of tongue twisters online, or just make up your own. For variation, try adding simple melodies.

Hot Spot

Good for: Loosening up, being silly, making associations

The players form a circle. One person jumps into the middle, picks any popular song, and starts singing it. The players who form the circle can sing along, if they want, while at the same time opening their minds to another song that has some kind of association to the song being sung. (There are no wrong associations with this warm-up.)

When a player on the outside of the circle gets an idea, he moves forward and taps out the person in the middle and starts singing a new, loosely related song. Similar to the pace of Freeze Tag and other fast-moving games, the person in the middle should never be out there too long.

To give you an example, the song associations might go something like this: "Light My Fire" (The Doors) – "You Light Up My Life" (Debby Boone) – "In My Life" (The Beatles) – "Livin' La Vida Loca" (Ricky Martin) – "Crazy" (Patsy Cline) – "Crazy on You" (Heart).

Association Rhymes

Good for: rhyming, making quick mental associations, rhythm, not thinking ahead

Everyone stands in a circle. The group taps to a mid-tempo beat. Then, one at a time going around the circle, a person says a rhyme in time with the rhythm.

Start by resting on the first and second beats, then say the word and it's rhyme on the third and fourth beats. Then the next person comes up with any word they associate with the last rhyme (again, no association is wrong) and makes their own rhyme, using the same rhythmic structure.

It might go something like this:

/ / dog – frog

/ / marsh – harsh

/ / mean – green

/ / leaf – grief

To add variation, you can change where the rhymes fall (on the second and third beats, for example). Or go faster and faster, or play it as an elimination game. The important thing with this one is that everyone does their best to stay in time.

My Name Is

Good for: rhyming, rhythm, working as a team

Improvisers love warming up in a circle, and this exercise is no exception. Again, establish a beat. The first person "introduces" themselves in four beats. Then, go around the circle as each player uses the same rhythmic pattern the first person established.

Remind whoever starts that it's important to think of a name that's easy to rhyme with, so everyone in the circle can use a different rhyming word. One-syllable names are easier, of course.

If someone can't think of a rhyme when it's their turn, they can just repeat the same name established at the beginning. The goal is for everyone to stay in time, and to get all the way around the circle.

It might go like this:

Player 1: My name is Bob

Player 2: I'm in the mob

Player 3: I am a slob

Player 4: My corn's on cob

If you really want to stretch, let everyone have eight beats instead of four. This allows each player to get more of the story out.

Example:

Player 1: Hey everybody / my name is Bob

Player 2: I live with my parents / I don't have a job

If you want to get really advanced, give a full 16 beats to each person. They'll be able to tell even more of the story, with the rhyming word still placed at the very end of their line.

Player 1: Listen up students / I am your teacher /
I love economics / my name is Bob

Player 2: I eat at restaurants / all of the time /
I like Thai food / especially mee krob

Again, use these warm-up exercises as a starting point. They've worked well over the years for Laura. Feel free to adapt them to your style and the singers you work with. Create your own unique warm-ups that loosen up your players and help them get grounded in rhythm, rhyme, emotional expression, and vocal projection.

Whose Line cast at the London Palladium (left to right): Josie Lawrence, Brad Sherwood, Colin Mochrie, Laura Hall, Clive Davis, Linda Taylor, Jeff Davis, and Greg Proops

Laura during a taping of *Whose Line*, with Drew Carey at the desk

Section 4

Working with Singers and Groups

You've made a lot of progress so far as you've worked your way through this book. Great job.

In this section we'll dig deeper into how you can help your players and support their individual needs. We'll also cover some useful advice if you are a singer or simply want to coach a singer with some best practices.

Finally, you'll get our best advice on how to be a team player in an improv group, along with some important etiquette do's and don'ts.

How to Adapt to Your Singers

As you work with an improv group for a while, you'll get to know your singers better. Over time you'll become familiar with their weaknesses and strengths. Once you have a handle on the cast's skill level, you can cater to individual player's musical needs.

For example, let's say you have an improviser who is not as strong musically as some of the other players. (We'll call him "Molin Dochrie.") You'll want to help him as much as you can by using simpler chord progressions and rhythms, clear bass movement from one chord to another, strong use of chords to indicate turnarounds, and less embellishment.

(Don't get the wrong idea. This fictional Molin character is a fine, upstanding individual. He just needs a little extra care in the singing department.)

However, in this same group of players you may have a strong singer who is much more versatile. (Let's call him "Blayne Grady.") With him you can get more complex, add embellishments, be more subtle in your chord progressions, and use intricate structural elements like pre-choruses, modulations and bridges.

No matter what the skill level of your group, you should always embrace all of your players, no matter how much they fit the sound of a traditional "singer." You may notice that some improvisers talk through songs more than they sing them (such as our fictional friend

Molin). But these talking singers can be every bit as funny as a player who belts out notes like a pro.

So stay aware of who you are supporting musically, love them all, and give them each what they need to look good onstage.

Laura on supporting the unique abilities of her veteran singers ...

Here's what I've learned about some of the singing improvisers I've played with the most.

Chip Esten likes clean, elegant song structures, while Jeff Davis likes to be surprised with the unusual.

Wayne Brady telegraphs a lot physically, so I've learned it's best to really keep an eye on him.

Kathy Kinney loves to sing, but she prefers to do it more organically in scenes than in structured games. So I try to give her the chance by playing underscore chords that can turn into a song if she chooses.

Greg Proops doesn't get to sing much, but he has a vast knowledge of music. So if anyone is going to laugh at a musical reference I play, it'll be him.

And, just so you know, none of the Whose Line *cast members likes doing "Hoedown"!*

Matching singers with styles

You will find that different singers are more comfortable with certain musical styles and feels. As the musician, you want to support your players in ways that will allow them to shine.

When playing a specific musical style, remember that you generally want to mimic the stereotypical sound of that style. You're not trying to forge a brand new sound that will win you a Grammy. You ideally want to play something that sounds familiar to the audience. What makes each song truly unique (and hopefully funny) are the spontaneous lyrics and the context in which it's sung.

When viewed in this light, some of your player's voices will be better suited to some genres more than others. One may do great with an old-fashioned country song but struggle with a Latin groove. Another might tear it up on a power ballad but fall apart when asked to freestyle over a hip-hop beat.

On one hand, you want to challenge your singers and help them grow. On the other hand, you don't want to put them in performance situations where they may feel like failures.

However, there are situations in shows where having an improviser sing something that is clearly out of their comfort zone can get a huge laugh. (Imagine if Molin Dochrie was forced to rap. That would be hilarious.)

Do your best to support your individual players as you encourage them to be ready for anything.

Choosing keys and keeping things simple

If you're working with a group of singers you don't know well, you'll probably want to start simple and pay close attention to their individual singing skills. You can always get more complex as you go, if they're up for it.

Laura has some go-to keys she likes to start with when she works with a new group of singers. Most women do well in the keys of Bb and C. These keys help them avoid going into a "head voice" if they don't want to. A lot of men sing well in D and E, since melodies in these keys are usually not too high or low for most guys.

That being said, with most improvised songs the singer can choose their own melody. So, no matter what key you play in, you should encourage players to pick a melody that lies comfortably within their range. Of course, some singers will be more adept at intuitively finding melodies than others.

We stressed this earlier, but it's worth repeating: The more musicians and/or singers involved in a song, the clearer and cleaner you want to keep things. Simple forms, clear rhythms, and clean chord progressions are going to help everyone stay together and sound good. Remember, you're the conductor of the train, so you want to make sure everyone is on board.

Laura on getting the *Whose Line* gig ...

I auditioned for Whose Line Is It Anyway? *with Brad Sherwood and Wayne Brady. I'd worked with Brad a few times prior but had never* met Wayne. I only slightly knew the producers, because they had asked me to play "Hoedown" dozens of times for the "cattle call" auditions. But now I was in the unique position of having to audition and earn my spot too.

I was asked to meet the British producers at a trendy Hollywood hotel. I remember waiting in the lobby with my gear. The place was so hip I couldn't tell whether the abstract, blob-like objects scattered around the lobby were sculptures or chairs.

Surprisingly, the audition was not held in a meeting room, as I had expected, but in the producer's hotel room. Hmm ... Here I was in a swanky room with three or four guys I barely knew. But it was all on the up and up, although it was a little weird for us to play and sing away in a hotel room.

The producers threw a lot of different styles at us. Brad and Wayne took turns and harmonized like they'd been singing together for years. Both were very funny, and we all listened to each other well, as all good improvisers should. Not everything we did that day was brilliant, but we made each other look good, and all three of us got hired.

I was certainly nervous going in, and the unusual setting didn't help any. But at one point I just stopped and told myself, "I know how to do this. I've done it for years!" I hardly ever feel that way at auditions.

It was a good reminder that when and if you get that lucky break, it really helps if you are prepared!

Tips for Singers

If you're a singer or an improv actor wanting some best practices on doing musical improv, this chapter is for you. If you're an improv musician, director, teacher or coach, you'll want to read this too.

Obviously, this book is about the role that music plays in supporting an improv comedy group and is primarily geared toward musicians. But we know a lot of non-musicians will read it too. With that in mind, we'd like to offer some of our top tips for singers.

If you are an improv group's musician, that doesn't necessarily mean you'll be the one to coach your singers. If your group has a music director or leader, defer to them for guidance. They may have a preference for who gives advice to the players. However, if you are in a new or smaller group, the actors may very well look to you for direction. After all, you are the music guy or gal.

The sensitive art of singing

The first thing you must realize is that improv actors will display a wide range of attitudes – and even strong emotions – related to musical improv.

You'll find veteran actors who brilliantly create dialogue and characters in their sleep but are terrified of singing. You'll also discover newbies who barely know the basics of improv but take to making up songs like they've been doing it for decades.

You'll find some players who love the challenge of rhyming and others who excel at organic songs that aren't dependent on rhymes. Some players are attracted to musical improv, while others are repelled by it. And all the while, many of them will deal with the ultimate improv F-word: FEAR!

Whether you are a singer yourself or just the musician or coach, love them (and yourself) through it. Offer encouragement and do your best to drown out that inner voice so many people have that says "I can't sing."

Another reason musical improv is so challenging for singers is because of all the things your brain has to juggle simultaneously: The notes you hit, the melody you sing, the rhythm and phrasing you use, the words you choose, the emotion you communicate ... and sometimes you have to rhyme too!

No wonder so many improv actors want to avoid it. But, as you know, that avoidance is keeping them (and perhaps you?) from some magically sweet moments onstage.

Let's talk

Here are some quick best practices when dealing with singing and singers:

Do you have a player who can't carry a tune or sing on key? Ask them to rhythmically speak their lines instead. Remember our friend Molin Dochrie? (Although Molin can actually carry a tune quite well when he has to.)

Good musical improv isn't always about singing beautifully. This isn't a talent contest. It's simply about expressing yourself musically and/or rhythmically. And many entertaining improvisers do that without singing a note.

In fact, some players find comfort in playing with an emotion or a character over music. It can actually be more compelling, partly because the music gives the scene an emotional underpinning.

Bob on using emotions and musical theatre ...

With a semi-structured song or organic musical scene, it's best to sing about the feeling or emotion in that moment, instead of using the song to move the plot forward.

Think about how songs are used in musical theatre productions. Usually a character has some new awareness or some plot twist has just occurred. The song is used to express how the character is dealing with the new situation.

In fact, I urge my singers to mimic that musical theatre style when doing organic song scenes. That means taking your time to let the chords play before you start singing. It means moving around the stage as your character sings – even if some of your verses are directed toward another player onstage with you.

You've probably heard of the term "talking heads" used as a general no-no. You usually want some movement onstage, not just two actors yapping. The same can be said for "singing heads." Try not to stand in one place as you sing your lines. You can even ham this up in some instances and use overly melodramatic gestures as you move.

Another cool thing you can borrow from musical theatre is to talk some of your lines and sing others. Move back and forth between talking and singing. There are no set rules for how to do this. Just let the emotion of the moment guide you.

All together now!

This was covered in Section 2, but it deserves repeating here. You can always spice up a song by creating a repeating refrain or chorus. Sometimes this tagline will be subtle; other times it can be used as a big sing-along anthem, ideally at the end of a scene or show.

That means singers don't have to come up with endless new verses. Keeping things simple and repetitive works too. In fact, in most instances, simple is best.

Laura on knowing when to rhyme ...

One of the big stumbling blocks for a lot of improvisers is rhyming. When I teach workshops I always talk about when to rhyme and when to not worry about it. With song games like "Hoedown" or "Irish Drinking Song," obviously you have to rhyme, using a very specific rhyme scheme. But in less-structured games, like Three-Headed Broadway Star or That Sounds Like a Song (aka Sing It), you can rhyme as little or as much as you want.

When singing organically in scenes, the most important things you can focus on are being in character, expressing emotion, and having a distinct point of view. You can take comfort in being guided by the same principles that apply to improv acting. It's just that you deliver your lines melodically and with accompaniment.

Rhyming with yourself and other players

Coming up with verses that rhyme in the moment is tricky enough. Things get even more interesting when you realize that sometimes you create all the rhymes yourself, while other times you have to rhyme with other players.

For instance, the way that "Hoedown" is usually played, each singer gets to make up an entire verse on their own, using what's called an A-A, B-B rhyming scheme.

Here's an example using "dog walking" as the audience suggestion:

My best friend is a dog, his name is Rin Tin Tin

He is like my family, a furry next of kin

When I take him for a walk, I pray to the Lord

That he doesn't pop a squat, in my neighbor's yard

As you can see, the first two lines end with one rhyming sound. The second two lines end with a different rhyming sound. And, as the singer, you get to enjoy the challenge of coming up with all four lines on your own. (Note that "Lord" and "yard" are "soft" rhymes, and those are perfectly fine.)

With the game "Irish Drinking Song," four singers typically have to rhyme with each other. On *Whose Line*, they sing very short verse snippets, which is quite challenging. We'll give you an altered version that's a bit easier for most singers. Here's an example using "Bill the plumber" as the suggestion:

Player 1: Oh, Bill he was a plumber, he liked to work with pipes.

Player 2: He would always get upset, and fill the air with gripes.

Player 3: One day he felt depressed, and got into a rut.

Player 4: Then he bought a new belt, and lost his plumber's butt.

"Irish Drinking Song" also uses an A-A, B-B rhyming scheme, but the verses are split among all the singers. Plus, this tune moves pretty quickly, so you have to be on your toes.

Regardless of whether you rhyme with yourself or with another player, you must train your brain to quickly brainstorm words that sound alike. That's where the rhyming warm-up exercises in the previous section can really help.

Another way to make it easy on yourself and your fellow players: Use simple, common, one-syllable words when setting up rhymes. Words like car, dog and bat are much easier to rhyme with, compared to purple, orange or perpendicular (although it can be fun for the audience to watch you struggle with more complex words every now and then).

Bob on his rhyming technique ...

This is a more advanced rhyming trick, but it has really helped me and other improv singers I've shared it with. When I'm doing a song that involves me rhyming with myself – such as the A-A, B-B verses in "Hoedown" – I like to choose what word I will end with first.

As soon as I know the topic, I start mentally running through funny references I might want to end the verse with. One time I sang a doo-wop song about popcorn. I quickly decided to end the verse with a reference to the kernels getting stuck in my teeth.

Once I chose "teeth," I had to think of a word that sounds like teeth to set up the rhyme. I came up with "grief." Then I launched into the song, not even knowing what the first two lines would be. Here's what I sang:

I like my popcorn, it tastes so good

It goes down easy, like a cheap snack should

One thing I don't like, it can cause me grief

When those damn kernels, get stuck in my teeth

Why do I take this "start from the end" approach? I'd rather have a so-so beginning and end the verse strong, as opposed to having a funny opening line that peters out at the end.

Of course, all of these mental gymnastics have to happen quickly. If this trick helps you, go for it. Otherwise, just start singing the first thing that comes to mind, and trust that you'll discover the right words along the way.

Practice and learn

This subject is obviously much bigger than this one chapter can cover. Luckily, there are several good books on the subject, some of which we list in the Improv Resources chapter in Section 5. Also, a growing number of improv groups and teachers offer classes on musical improv. Plus, you can always get Laura's *Improv Karaoke* CDs and hone your skills by singing along with them.

Laura and Rick Hall with workshop students from the Arcade Theater in Pittsburgh

How to Be a Good Team Player

Being part of an improv group (like being part of a band, sports team, or marriage) can be some of the most fun you'll ever have. However, since you're dealing with other human beings, it can also be challenging. Getting all the big personalities of an improv group to work together in harmony can be difficult, but it's also part of what makes a group interesting.

Laura on Chris Farley and what you bring to the table ...

I did a few shows on the road with Chris Farley during my time at The Second City. He was so talented and could be really fun. But I also describe him as a "sweet mess." Because of the internal issues he wrestled with, he was sadly inconsistent, unreliable and volatile. Even though he was incredibly talented, and I know he had a good heart, it was difficult at times to be on an improv team with him.

Some of the best advice I got as a young musician was this: There are lots of talented people out there, and your musical abilities are only one part of why people want to work with you. So, besides working on your musical chops, also strive to be helpful and prepared. Become a responsible and reliable team member. Be a good person to hang out with.

This is especially important if you go on the road together. Be as positive and considerate as you can to your fellow players. But also take care of yourself so you can bring your best work every chance you get.

Know your offstage role

If there are any problems onstage or off, do your best to listen and communicate clearly. Pointing fingers or blaming people rarely helps a situation get better, and oftentimes makes it worse. Avoid gossiping, complaining or attempting to divide the group into factions. And don't ever try to work out issues after the show when you've all had a few drinks. Wait for the light of day, when your heads will be clearer.

Also, know your role within the group. Is there a director, founder or leader of your team? If so, respect that person's position and know that the final word always rests with them. Even if you don't agree with everything they do, the leader has the final say. You can make suggestions, and hopefully the person in charge will be open to hearing feedback, but refrain from getting upset if your ideas aren't automatically accepted.

What if you are the founder or leader? What's your leadership style? Do your players feel they have a say in what games are played, added and performed? As the leader, are you organized and clear? Do you delegate and give every player an opportunity to shine? Do you dish out lots of compliments? Are you thoughtful and sensitive when providing feedback?

Team leaders should strike a balance between consensus and decision-making. It's great to ask for opinions and be aware of how every player feels. But someone has to cast the final vote, and that job goes to the director, founder or improv team leader.

Laura on dating group members ...

I want to warn you to be cautious about dating other team members. If the relationship goes well, be careful not to become a "block of two" that bullies the other members.

If the relationship goes sour, try not to air your dirty laundry in front of the rest of the group. And if things get really ugly, it may end up being impossible for you to be on the same team together.

That being said, I met my husband when we improvised together in The Second City Touring Company, and he's the love of my life. So it can work out. Just be cautious.

Laura with Chip Esten from *Whose Line* and *Nashville*. Since these photos come right after a section on dating ... No, I never dated Chip, or Greg below. But they are great performer friends.

Laura with Greg Proops

Section 5

A Final Flurry of Musical Improv Goodness

We're almost to the end, but we're not done yet.

We know you've got burning questions for Laura about her *Whose Line* experiences, and she's got answers galore.

In addition, we'll give you a solid list of improv comedy resources to beef up your knowledge, as well as some final thoughts to send you on your way.

We'll also thank some important people and let you know how to reach us online.

Laura Answers Frequently Asked Questions About *Whose Line Is It Anyway?*

How do you keep from laughing on the show while you play?

People ask me this question the most. The truth is, when I'm in the middle of doing improv, I'm so focused I hear it in a different way than the audience does. I'm listening for the form, where the singers are going, what's happening next, etc. So it doesn't register as funny in the same way. But when I watch it on TV later, I laugh my butt off just like the rest of the audience.

What's your favorite memory of the show?

We were playing Three-Headed Broadway Star (also known as the One-Word-at-a-Time Song). It was going really well, we were all listening to each other and connecting, and we were heading into a big, emotional bridge.

Drew Carey got so swept away, he belted out, "Won't you take me on a …" before he realized he'd sung far more than one word. He started giggling (Drew's got the best laugh) and couldn't stop for the rest of the song. I loved that moment so much because it was so genuine.

What's your favorite improv game?

On *Whose Line* I really like playing Scene to Rap and Show Stopping Number. They're very similar in that during a scene the actors have to suddenly burst into song. I also love Three-Headed Broadway Star because it's a game where the singers can't think ahead, so it often ends up being quite random and silly.

How did Linda Taylor get on the show?

Linda auditioned and joined the show during our second season on ABC. She didn't have any previous improv experience, but she's played with lots of different people over the years. She is such a talented and flexible musician, she figured it out quickly.

Our musical backgrounds complement each other well. I'm more versed in styles like country, musical theater and jazz. She's got more chops in R&B, hip-hop and Motown. We didn't know each other before she started doing the show, but we've become good friends. We've worked together on lots of other projects too, including film scores. She also played on both albums by my band, The Sweet Potatoes.

Are you guys really improvising? How can everything be so funny?

Yes, we really do improvise! But remember, the show is also edited. For example, with the game Greatest Hits, they use two or three songs in the final episode, but we probably recorded five or six in the studio. They only include the best ones to air.

However, sometimes they'll include a terrible one, because it can also be fun to watch us crash and burn. But they usually cut out the inevitable mediocre games and songs.

Remember, the actors on the show are some of the best improvisers in the world, so we have a pretty good success rate. But even then, not everything is brilliant.

So you can take comfort in knowing that even the pros have scenes and songs that fall flat.

Why don't they let you improvise?

Honestly, this is the question I dislike the most. Why? Because it implies that what I do on the show isn't improvising and assumes I would rather be an actor/improviser than a musician/improviser. Make no mistake, I absolutely love what I do and have never once wished I was on the other side of the piano.

What's a *Whose Line* show recording day like?

Linda Taylor and I get to the studio around noon to test our gear, sound check, and warm up. Then we do camera blocking with the actors, mostly for the "fourth chair" person to know where to stand and which camera to look at for games like Weird News Casters, etc.

(In case you're wondering what the term "fourth chair" means, here's a quick explanation: For many years the main actors on *Whose Line* have been Colin, Ryan and Wayne. You can count on all three of them to be in most episodes. The fourth chair features a revolving door of great improvisers, many of whom were named earlier in the book.)

Around 4:00 PM we start hair, makeup and wardrobe, and then we have dinner. The studio audience is usually seated around 5:30. Before we start, Dan Patterson, the creator of the show, warms up the crowd and introduces the cast. Linda and I go out first and then play the rest of the players on.

It's a long night for the audience, cast and crew, usually going until 10:30 PM or so. But we have the best audiences, and they hang in there with us, even though they haven't had dinner and the studio air conditioning is set to "stun" (so the actors don't get hot running around under the lights).

In one five-hour night of recording, we usually perform 22 to 26 games. Five to eight of them include music. When we're not doing the music games, Linda and I hang out in our own little "clubhouse" backstage and watch the show on a monitor. The space actually resembles a small storage room, where we do glamorous things like tweet and touch up our lipstick. During the break, Linda and I go out and jam, which I especially love to do.

The producers always get at least two shows out of each night of taping, and sometimes three. On some occasions they get four! Because of this we can get a whole season recorded quickly. In 2016, for example, we got at least 24 episodes out of ten recording days. Compare that to most sitcoms, which shoot for five full days to get one episode.

While we're recording on any given night, the producers think about which games will go together to make up each episode. After we've played all the games, they go back and record a few show openings and closings with host Aisha Tyler. They also record dozens of transition segments, going to and coming out of commercials, introducing games, etc. Having all these editing options helps the producers stitch together the episodes.

How is being on the CW Network different than being on ABC?

All of the episodes with Drew Carey aired on ABC. The new version, with host Aisha Tyler, is on the CW.

Because ABC was a more family-oriented channel, the show had to be a lot cleaner, so questionable lines and gestures got censored out. But on the CW, the host and actors can get away with a lot more.

Personally, I don't think the looser rules are necessarily better. Don't get me wrong, I'm not a prude. But when you have to do a cleaner show, it can challenge you to be more clever and creative.

Plus, young adults often come up to me and say, "I've loved *Whose Line* since I was a kid. My whole family watched it together." That makes me really happy!

What were some of your favorite celebrity appearances?

I was thrilled to meet Sid Caesar. Being one of the pioneers of television comedy, he was a historic figure to me. Plus, he was a perfect gentleman, charming and a bit flirty – a winning combination. I also loved meeting Florence Henderson, who I grew up watching on *The Brady Bunch*. She was the ideal TV mom and so gracious in person.

The wildest ones were definitely Robin Williams and Richard Simmons. Robin's brain went a mile a minute, and Richard was like a ping-pong ball bouncing out of control. They both kept everyone on their toes.

How does Aisha Tyler compare to Drew Carey as host?

Different people have their favorites, but I think they're both fantastic. Both of them are quick, super smart, and want to make sure everyone around them is having a good time. So, although they have different personalities, cultural references, styles, etc., they both exude ideal qualities as hosts.

What has *Whose Line* done for your career?

For a television show, *Whose Line* has had an incredibly long run. Not only did we have a great eight-year run on ABC, but as of 2016, we're into our fourth year on the CW. Plus, there have been a lot of live performances over the years in many configurations with different cast members. I'm incredibly grateful for all the work the show has provided me.

Of course, the show has helped me get my foot into lots of doors, and I'm thankful for that too. But the truth is, in different musical areas – such as booking my band, scoring films, teaching, etc. – although I may have a foot in the door, I still have to prove myself in the new context.

Have you collaborated with any other well-known musicians on improv shows?

When we were doing *Whose Line* on ABC, we did a lot of live shows billed as Drew Carey's Improv All Stars. We even did a USO tour in the Middle East. We also played in Las Vegas every year during Super Bowl weekend.

Drew, who knows a lot of people, is friends with Joe Walsh, the renowned guitar player from the Eagles. One year Drew invited Joe to come to Vegas and play with us. Joe Walsh! Sitting in with Linda and me! I was rather star struck, to say the least.

But here's the funny thing: Joe called me before we did the shows. He had never done improv and wanted to learn more about the format. He asked if we could meet up, play together, and work on a few styles.

So one day Joe Walsh shows up on my doorstep, ready for me to teach him about musical improv! It felt so weird that he wanted me to help him.

But then I realized, even though he's a fantastic musician and obviously knows how to improvise in the context of a band, this kind of improv is completely different. Joe was entering a new arena and he wanted to do the best job possible.

Even though it felt strange to be telling him what to do, I admired his sense of being a student, ready to learn.

So if a superstar like Joe Walsh knows he needs to learn the specialized art of playing music to support an improv group, you shouldn't feel too bad about needing to study and practice yourself.

By the way, the highpoint of the Vegas shows for me that year was being on stage with Joe playing the opening riff to "Life's Been Good" and hearing the crowd go wild.

Laura with Joe Walsh in Las Vegas, 2011

Improv Resources

There are a lot of great books, websites, schools, and resources that are available to teach and enlighten you about improv – far too many to list them all.

But here's a rundown of some of our favorites ...

Books for musicians

Musical Direction for Improv and Sketch Comedy by Michael Pollack

The Contemporary Keyboardist - Stylistic Etudes by John Novello

Hal Leonard Pocket Music Theory: A Comprehensive and Convenient Source for All Musicians by Carl Schroeder and Keith Wyatt

Music Theory Workbook for All Musicians by Chris Bowman

Chord Progressions: Theory and Practice by Dan Fox and Dick Weissman

Improv resources for singers

Improv Karaoke, Vol. 1 and Vol. 2 by Laura Hall and Luke Hannington

Instant Songwriting: Musical Improv from Dunce to Diva by Nancy Howland Walker

Musical Improv Comedy: Creating Songs in the Moment by Michael Pollack

Books on improv acting and history

Improvise: Scene From the Inside Out by Mick Napier

Upright Citizens Brigade Comedy Improvisation Manual by Matt Walsh

Improvising Better: A Guide for the Working Improviser by Jimmy Carrane and Liz Allen

Impro: Improvisation and the Theatre by Keith Johnstone

Something Wonderful Right Away: An Oral History of The Second City and the Compass Players by Jeffrey Sweet

Books on long form

Truth in Comedy: The Manual for Improvisation by Charna Halpern, Del Close, and Kim "Howard" Johnson

Behind the Scenes: Improvising Long Form by Mick Napier

Improv websites

Improv Nerd with Jimmy Carrane
www.JimmyCarrane.com/improv-nerd-podcast/

Improv Encyclopedia
www.ImprovEncyclopedia.org

Kevin Mullaney
www.KevinMullaney.com

People and Chairs
www.PeopleAndChairs.com

Final Thoughts

You've made it to the end of the book. Congratulations! You've got a head full of new improv insights and musical best practices.

Now what?

The next thing you should do is get out there and do it. Dive in. Make the leap. Take action.

Over time, you will develop an approach that works for you, even if it feels like you're fumbling around in the beginning. You'll become part of the fabric of whatever group or groups you work with. After a while, they'll never want to play without you. You might even become an in-demand musician in your local improv community and beyond.

If you get only one thing out of this book, just know that playing for improv is actually about doing less rather than more. It's about playing simply and clearly, especially when you accompany singers. It's about the magic of leading and following at the same time ... and creating something amazing out of thin air with your teammates.

Okay, that's more than one thing, but you know what we mean.

Now go and have fun spreading laughter to as many people as possible!

Laura on reaching a major milestone …

When I was on the road with Drew Carey's Improv All Stars, we played Carnegie Hall. Yes, that Carnegie Hall. You know, the one that most musicians dream of. I think we may have been the first improv group to perform there.

The minute I entered through the stage door, I was reminded of this historic venue's significance. Pictures of past performers lined the hallways, the green room, even the backstage bathroom.

The Carnegie Hall staff and crew are incredibly proud of the space. They made me aware of several amazing musicians who had played the very piano I was about to play, including Glenn Gould, Sergei Rachmaninoff, George Gershwin, Count Basie, and Oscar Peterson – iconic pianists I'd studied in music school.

No pressure there, right? The crew didn't intend to intimidate me, but since I was already nervous, it did the trick.

As I put on my makeup in my dressing room, I had a silent talk with myself: "I know how to do this. All I have to do is stay in the moment, trust my fellow improvisers, and let it happen."

In honor of the venue, we decided to put the game Make an Opera into the set list. It's always been one of my favorite games because it can flow so freely musically, and the emotions are often heightened because of the nature of the genre.

When we played the game that night, it suddenly struck me as hilarious that we were making up an opera on the same stage where

Maria Callas and Luciano Pavarotti had sung "real" opera. It filled my heart with joy and delight.

What a strange career this has been – an endless series of delightful surprises. I hope improv becomes a great source of joy for you too, wherever it takes you.

Laura on stage at Carnegie Hall in 2011.

Acknowledgements

Laura

I want to thank all of the people who helped me grow as an improvising musician. Luckily, I got to learn from the best. First and foremost, the amazing Fred Kaz, who was such a great mentor and example to me.

I've learned so much from working and being friends with directors Ron West, Jane Morris, Mick Napier, Tom Booker, and Shulie Cowen. A big shout out goes to talented musicians such as Lisa McQueen (whose thorough and thoughtful notes made this a much better book), Faith Soloway, and my partner in crime on *Whose Line*, Linda Taylor. Thanks to my lovely sister, Leslie Wasserman, for her help with editing.

I also want to acknowledge my crazy, funny family. Our lives are one big improvisation; we're making it up as we go. And, of course, loads of thanks to Bob Baker, who inspired me to think and write about this seemingly impossible thing I've been doing all these years.

Bob

I'd like to thank my friend Toni McMurphy, who in 2011 challenged me to get back into improv (and start teaching it) after years of hearing me talk about it. That was the serious nudge I needed. And look what it led to! A big heap of gratitude to Marigene DeRusha for giving me a space to teach and perform in and being such a supportive cheerleader.

Thanks to Suz Doyle for all the detailed improv notes and Jennifer Stolzer for help with the cover art. And thanks to Pooki for the unwavering love and support you give me.

A big round of applause to the vibrant St. Louis improv community and everyone who has ever attended one of my classes or performed in an Improv Comedy Cabaret show. You know who you are. I appreciate you more than you'll ever know.

Thanks especially to Laura Hall, for trusting me to help communicate your life's work in improv. I couldn't ask for a better co-author.

Bob with the Playback Theatre group (left to right): Howie Hirshfield, Theresa Masters, Clayton Bury, Tamira Christensen, Denise Saylor, Joan Lipkin, Nancy Nigh, Cammie Middleton-Helmsing, and Bob Baker

How to Connect with Laura and Bob

Find out more about Laura at **www.LauraHall.com**

(While you're on the website, I'd love it if you joined my mailing list. I'll keep you updated about workshops, live shows, *Whose Line*, and more.)

Learn more about *Improv Karaoke* at **www.ImprovKaraoke.com**

For info on Laura's band, The Sweet Potatoes, visit **www.TheSweetPotatoes.com**

You'll also find Laura on ...

www.Twitter.com/LauraHallMusic

www.Facebook.com/LauraHall

www.Facebook.com/TheSweetPotatoes

www.YouTube.com/TheSweetPotatoes

To contact Laura by email: **laura@laurahall.com**

For info on Bob's improv comedy drop-in classes and shows in the St. Louis area, visit **www.ImprovSTL.com**

For tips and tools on marketing for musicians, visit **www.TheBuzzFactor.com**

For more details about Bob's books, music, art and more, visit **www.Bob-Baker.com**

Some of Bob's other books include:

Guerrilla Music Marketing Handbook: 201 Self-Promotion Ideas for Songwriters, Musicians and Bands on a Budget

The Empowered Artist: A Call to Action for Musicians, Writers, Visual Artists, and Anyone Who Wants to Make a Difference With Their Creativity

55 Ways to Promote and Sell Your Book on the Internet

You'll also find Bob on ...

www.Twitter.com/MrBuzzFactor

www.YouTube.com/MrBuzzFactor

www.Facebook.com/BobBakerFanPage

www.instagram.com/mrbuzzfactor

To contact Bob by email: **bob@bob-baker.com**

Made in the USA
Monee, IL
26 October 2023

45257690R00090